The
Speech Title
Cookbook

Proven Recipes for Speech and Seminar Titles That Sell

Sam Wieder

The Speech Title Cookbook
Proven Recipes for Speech and Seminar Titles that Sell
By Sam Wieder

New Energy Dynamics
Post Office Box 963
Greensburg, PA 15601

Printed in the United States of America

Library of Congress Cataloging-in-Publication Data

Wieder, Sam
The speech title cookbook: proven recipes for speech and seminar titles that sell/by Sam Wieder—1st ed.
ISBN: 978-1-892241-01-6

Contents

No one who achieves success does so without acknowledging the help of others.

—*Alfred North Whitehead*

Acknowledgments

As I wrote this book, I examined the kinds of titles that have worked so well for many other speakers and writers and then figured out the recipes or formulas they used, either consciously or unconsciously, to create those titles. So I must first acknowledge all of the speakers and marketing professionals who have crafted the many effective titles I've come across over the years, providing me with such rich material for my analysis.

Additionally, several key individuals were of great help to me in moving this project forward and making my words more palatable to my intended reader. In particular, I'd like to thank Bonnie Budzowski, a book coach, friend, and fellow National Speakers Association member, who opened my mind to some creative possibilities in the early stages of my writing process and helped me to get out of my own way to finish writing this book. I must also thank Stella Togo, another publishing professional who helped me to embrace a bigger vision for this book and see what steps I would need to take to bring it into the world.

Communication coach Hank Walshak and marketing expert David Newman graciously shared their input on my book concept and title from a marketing perspective.

Long-time Toastmasters International member and master speech evaluator Mike Dalton offered his invaluable feedback to help me add greater clarity and precision to my opening chapters. David Piper, another early reader and reviewer, drew upon his outside-the-box thinking to help me see other areas for improvement.

I am also most thankful to my niece Megan Wieder, a talented cook and award-winning writer, who proofread this book and shared her insightful feedback.

In addition, I must credit my late wife, Dr. Jacqueline Paltis, for being the inspiration behind my framing this speech title guide as a cook book. As the author of the Sugar Control Bible and Cookbook, Jacqueline has shown thousands of people how to eat in a way that supports vibrant health. My greatest hope is for this book to be equally successful in showing speakers how to craft speech, seminar, and teleclass titles that are zesty and full of life.

Preface

If you are a professional who wants to speak to groups, you need to answer one or both of these two key questions:

1) How do I attract the attention of meeting and event planners who can book me to speak?
2) How do I motivate members of my ideal target audience to attend my presentation?

The "how" of making these things happen starts with your presentation title. This is the first thing that people see when they read about your program. It is also what they use to immediately gauge their level of interest.

If your title doesn't hook them, you may lose them altogether. But if your title grabs them, you are half way there. So your speech title, in essence, is the magic key that can open the door to a kingdom of exciting speaking opportunities and eager audiences.

Given this, I am amazed at the number of weak, bland, and unappetizing speech titles that I see, titles that utterly fail to engage the reader, even someone who could greatly benefit from the presentation. It is almost like having a delicious gourmet meal and then calling it gruel.

Seeing such a great need for guidance, I began to lay out some fundamental principles that my speech coaching clients could apply to create a compelling speech title. At first, I thought that I could sufficiently address this topic in a short article or booklet. I soon discovered, however, that it wasn't that simple.

Yes, there are some fundamentals you must grasp to create a compelling speech title. But beyond that, there is a wide variety of ways to design and structure a speech title—and many finer points involved in taking a title from good to great.

It then struck me that to convey all of this, I really needed to write a cook book of sorts. What I wanted to share, after all, were many recipes for crafting an effective speech title. The result? This book.

While this book is entitled "The Speech Title Cook Book," you can naturally apply its tactics and insights to create a compelling title for most any type of spoken or written work. This includes articles, books, e-books, marketing brochures, proposals, CD's, DVD's, workshops, seminars, teleclasses, webinars, and whatever information form the next wave of technology may bring.

Whatever way you want to share your expertise, you will find in these pages the guidance and inspiration you need to brand it with a title that will command your market's attention. With just a measure of helpful cooking advice and a dollop of your own creativity, you can soon make people hungry for all that you have to offer.

Introduction

Put on Your Chef's Hat

Unlike a typical cook book, this one doesn't require you to have a stove, a collection of cooking utensils, and a selection of foods and spices. Your desire to write a compelling speech title will provide the heat. The only utensils you need are a pen and paper or a computer, if you prefer. Your mind and imagination will generate all of the needed ingredients—the ideas, words, and phrases you can combine to cook up a taste-tempting title.

Of course, you will need to be able to follow a recipe and willing to exercise some creativity in applying what you learn to craft a title that works for you. If that's the case, though, this cook book will provide the insights and guidance you need to start cooking up some savory speech titles in no time.

To help spark your creativity, I offer a variety of sample titles for each recipe. While each example is designed to demonstrate the key elements of a particular recipe, it is by no means offered as an ideal speech title for a certain topic. What makes a speech title ideal is not merely the design but also how well the title conveys a presentation's focus and connects with the speaker's target audience.

So if you are tempted to just use one of the sample titles that relate to your topic, that won't necessarily produce miraculous results for you. Using sample speech titles as models, you really need to step back and assess how you can best apply each recipe to your particular situation.

What do you most want to say in your title to capture the essence of your presentation? How can you say it so that your target audience truly gets it? By bringing your answers to these questions into your creative cooking process, you will achieve the best possible results.

This is also the difference between cooks who simply follow a recipe and those who develop the artistry of a master chef. The true cooking artists use a recipe as a foundation, but they are also willing to experiment and explore new possibilities. They will consider the context or occasion for a meal. They will play with different flavor combinations. They will tailor a recipe to match the tastes of those who will dine on their culinary creations.

My hope is that this book will guide and inspire you to embrace the mindset and spirit of a master chef. If it does, you will find yourself cooking up presentation titles that will help you to land more speaking engagements and consistently attract a crowd to your speeches, workshops, teleclasses, and webinars.

So what are we waiting for? Let's get cooking!

Part One

Prep Work for a Savory Speech Title

He who is best prepared can best serve
his moment of inspiration.

—*Samuel Taylor Coleridge*

Chapter One

Alphabet Soup:
The ABC's of Clarity

Master chefs know that the creation of a great meal starts with proper planning and preparation. This critical element of meal preparation is sometimes referred to by the French phrase "mise en place," which translates into "putting in place." In professional kitchens, this means the organizing of the ingredients and equipment needed for the menu items that are being prepared.

To create a tantalizing speech title, you must also begin with "mise en place." For you, this involves clarifying and putting in place a few key ingredients.

These ABC's of clarity include:

1) **A**udience – Who is your ideal target audience?
2) **B**enefit(s) – How will your target audience most benefit from your talk?
3) **C**hallenge(s) – What challenge or challenges will your talk help your audience members overcome?

The more clearly you define these elements at the start, the better. So let's take a closer look at each one.

Audience

New salespeople often make a common mistake. When first talking to a potential customer, they take little or no time to find out about their prospect's wants or needs. They just launch right into a sales pitch.

The result? Usually, they walk away without a sale. The reason is simple. Because they knew so little about their prospects, they were unable to frame their pitch in terms of their prospects needs and wants. In short, they didn't know their audience.

Your speech title is, in essence, a mini-sales-pitch for your speech. If you create your title without giving any real thought to your intended audience, you are no better off than a novice salesperson. You too, most likely, will fail to capture the attention and interest of those you most want to persuade.

Speakers often ask me what I think of their speech titles. Rather than immediately offer my opinion, I usually first respond with this question: Who is your target audience?" Without knowing that, I really can't offer any truly helpful feedback. I may love their speech title. But if I'm not a member of their target audience, my opinion may not be worth much.

To effectively evaluate a speech title, you need to look at it through the eyes of your intended audience. And to do that, you first need to have a clear idea of who will be in that audience.

You can start to define your ideal target audience by identifying its demographics. These are the common external characteristics of the people or businesses you most want to address. Demographic factors for individuals could include gender, age, marital status, ethnic background, education, occupation, and geographic location. Demographic factors for businesses might include industry, company size, number of years in business, stage of growth, workforce make-up, revenues, and type of customer served.

Once you have a clear demographic snapshot of your target audience, you can then identify its psychographics. These are the common internal characteristics of your ideal audience, their common values, beliefs and attitudes. Do they value freedom, honesty, achievement, relationships or helping others? Are they family-oriented, hard-working, innovative or passionate about making a difference in the world? If the audience is a business, does it value teamwork, initiative, and personal development?

Take a few minutes now and write down a demographic and psychographic profile of your target audience.

Benefits

The second step to prepare you for creating a winning speech title is to turn your attention to benefits. Not just any benefits. But the most important benefits your target audience will gain by hearing your presentation.

Now, you may be able to rattle off several benefits and think that you've done your job here. But there's a little more to it than that. To identify the benefits that have the most firepower, you really need to embrace the mindset of your target audience members and get a sense of what would be most helpful and useful to them out of all of the information you have to share.

Of course, this is much easier to do once you've created the demographic and psychographic profiles described above. So if you haven't done that yet for your target audience, now would be a great time. Even jotting down a couple of short profiles would be a good first step.

To identify the benefits that are most important to your target audience, begin by asking this question: "Within the scope of my topic, what does my target audience want most?" What do they most want to have? What do they most want to be able to do? How do they most want to be?

Once you've generated some solid answers to these questions, work on defining a much bigger and broader benefit known as an ideal outcome. This is a picture of how your target audience members would like their situation, their business, or their life to be if they could wave a magic wand and make anything happen. This may be a combination of the answers you gave when you looked at what they wanted to have, do, or be. It might even be something beyond all of that.

Let's say that you are a nutrition expert who speaks about healthy eating. Your target audience is busy professional women who often struggle to balance work and family life. Within the realm of health and nutrition, what do they want most? They want a satisfying diet that supports their health. They want to eat well, prepare nutritious meals for their family, and meet the demands of their busy lives. They want to look and feel great.

But let's go a step further. Beyond all of this, what might these professional women see as their ideal outcome? One strong possibility would be vibrant health for themselves and their families. Health, after all, is what enables them to meet life's challenges, seize life's opportunities, and create the lives they want.

How about the members of your target audience? What are their most compelling desires? In relation to your topic, what is their ideal outcome? These ripe, juicy desires are key ingredients you can fold into your speech title to make people hungry for your words of wisdom.

Challenges

Once you have defined your target audience and identified what it wants most, you are almost ready to start crafting your presentation title. What is still missing, though, is an ingredient that can take your title from good to great, from common to compelling, from ordinary to extraordinary. That missing ingredient is a deep sense of your audience's challenges and struggles.

What are your target audience members struggling with? What is making their lives difficult? What is keeping them from achieving what they want most? Understand this and you will have a zesty hot sauce to give your speech title recipe some real kick.

Consider, once again, the nutrition expert whose target audience is busy professional women. These women may ultimately want vibrant health for themselves and their families. Still, they may face a number of challenges that make it difficult for them to achieve that outcome.

Some possibilities:

- Little time to prepare healthy, nutritious meals
- Feeling too stressed to cook
- Addictions to certain unhealthy fast foods.
- Children who are hooked on junk food

Our nutrition expert could title her talk "How to Design a Healthy Diet," which could certainly have some appeal to her target audience. But because this title simply focuses on a general outcome, it will be lucky to generate a luke-warm response.

What might be possible, though, if she were to add a dash of the challenges faced by her target audience? Here is a sampling of titles that she might serve up:

- Healthy Eating When You're Pressed for Time
- How to Beat Stress by Eating Right
- Overcome the Fast Food Blues with Healthy Salads, Soups and Stews
- Getting Your Kids to Trash the Junk Food Habit

Notice the difference? These challenge-infused titles convey pressing issues of the speaker's target audience. As such, they are vitalized with real drawing power.

This isn't to say that every speech title should express an element of challenge. Sometimes the challenge or struggle can be implied and other times it may be most appropriate to craft a speech title that is totally focused on a positive outcome. In any case, you will be best prepared to create a winning speech title if you first understand your audience's most pressing problems and challenges.

Your ABC's Worksheet

Here is an ABC's worksheet to help you distill the ABC's of clarity for your target audience. Address each item in as much detail as possible. Just as a master chef ensures that he or she has all of the essential ingredients before starting to cook, so must you. Do this and you will have the needed stock or starter for a smorgasboard of tantalizing titles.

   I. Who is your target audience?

      A. External characteristics (such demographics as gender, age, marital status, ethnic background, education, occupation)

      B. Internal characteristics (values and beliefs)

  II. What benefits do your audience members want?

      A. What do they most want to have?

      B. What do they most want to be able to do?

      C. How do they most want to be?

      D. Ideally, how do they want their business, life, or situation to be different than it is now?

 III. What are their biggest challenges?

      A. What are they struggling with?

      B. What is making their life difficult?

      C. What is keeping them from achieving what they want most?

Conveying the ABC's of Clarity

Does your title clearly state or imply who your target *audience* is, how your listeners will *benefit* from your program and/or what pressing *challenge* of theirs that you will address?

See how these sample titles hit all of the marks.

How Financial Sales Professionals Can Overcome the Toughest Objections

Audience (stated): Financial Sales Professionals
Benefit (implied): More Sales
Challenge (stated): Overcoming Objections

Interviewing Techniques to Help You Identify Top-Level Managerial Talent

Audience (implied): Hiring Managers
Benefit (stated): Identifying top-level managerial talent
Challenge (implied): Finding great managers can be hard.

Beat Stress by Eating Right

Audience (implied): People who are stressed
Benefit (implied): Greater health and vitality
Challenge (stated): Beating stress

Chapter Two

Combine the Basic Ingredients

Once you have laid out the basic ingredients of your presentation title, your next step is to consider how you might refine and combine them. You have defined your target audience and identified its pressing problems and compelling desires. You have a presentation that will address those problems and desires. Now what?

As a starting point, create a working title that includes all 3 basic ingredients of audience, benefit, and challenge. To do this, follow this simple formula:

How A (audience) can overcome C (challenge) to achieve B (benefit/outcome)

Using our example from the first chapter, this might translate into:

How Professional Women Can Make Time in Their Busy Lives to Prepare Nutritious and Delicious Meals that Keep Them Healthy and Energetic

Yes, this working title is fairly long, unwieldy, and difficult to digest. To create this type of working title, however, you must more sharply define and express the 3 core ingredients of audience, benefit, and challenge. This, in turn, can spark your thinking about how you might convey these elements in a title that is much more catchy and compelling.

Here are a few more examples of this 3-ingredient working title:

- How Job Hunters Can Reduce Their Job Search Struggles and Land Promising Interviews
- How Managers Can Address Conflict in the Workplace and Create a Positive, Productive Working Environment
- How Salespeople Can Overcome Call Reluctance and Boost Their Sales Performance

Of course, none of these working titles will make it into the Speech Title Hall of Fame (if indeed such a hall exists). But we're not looking to craft an electrifying title in 20 seconds or less. The purpose of a working title is simply to offer a place to begin.

While this type of working title clearly expresses your basic ingredients of audience, benefit, and challenge, your final title may not even fully convey all of these elements in words. As you pare it down, your audience may be assumed or implied from the context of the title. For instance, if you are giving a talk about how to land a job interview, you wouldn't need to specify in your title that your program is for job hunters.

Sometimes the challenge or benefit may be clearly implied. If, for example, you're giving a talk entitled "How to Land a 6-Figure Contract," it is fairly self-evident that this would involve a real element of challenge. Or if you're giving a talk entitled "How to Overcome Stage Fright Once and for All," the benefit or outcome of self-confidence is also implied.

Once you start to experiment with different title possibilities using the recipes in this book, you will find various ways to tighten and strengthen your language. Depending upon your topic and audience, you may also find it helpful to highlight one of your 3 core ingredients or have it overshadow the others. In the coming chapters, you will learn specifically how to do this.

What you are striving to achieve as your final result is a title that contains the essence of your 3 core ingredients of audience, benefit, and challenge, whether or not all of these elements are explicitly expressed. While you may not be able to taste every ingredient that went into your favorite cake, each one played a role in creating the distinctive flavor that delights your taste buds. So it is with the core ingredients of a winning speech title.

Moving Beyond Your Working Title

So far in this chapter, we've looked at a basic format for combining 3 core ingredients of audience, benefit, and challenge into a working speech title. Admittedly, that working title will most likely be somewhat wordy and a bit awkward-sounding. But if creating it has done nothing more than to help you uncover what drives and motivates your target audience, then the effort was well worth it.

With that understanding, you will be able to consider many other ways of expressing and combining your core ingredients to create a title with real drawing power. Most of the rest of this book is devoted to helping you explore those possibilities.

As you experiment with these different methods of crafting a speech title, keep this in mind. Most presentation titles today actually consist of two components—a fairly short, catchy main title and a longer, more descriptive subtitle. This allows you to quickly grab people's attention with your title and then follow it up with a subtitle that more clearly conveys the value of your presentation.

A strong main title will also generally communicate plenty of value. Sometimes it may even be strong enough to stand alone. But when that's not the case, there's nothing quite like a title and subtitle that work in tandem to sell your speech.

With many of the speech title recipes in this book, you may want to think of the resulting title you create as being a subtitle. You can then develop a much more punchy and concise main title to complement it.

Of course, other recipes show you how to create those short, snappy titles. So in those cases, you could take a longer, more descriptive title you created with a different recipe and use that as your subtitle.

As you familiarize yourself with different recipes, you will find plenty of opportunities to mix and match. Have fun with this. The recipes will guide you in finding inventive ways of creating compelling speech titles. It is your imagination, though, that will take you to a whole new world of creative possibility.

Chapter Three

Cater to Your Audience

Did you ever notice how you perk right up whenever you hear someone say your name? Something similar may happen when you overhear a person talking about a situation that is similar to one you've experienced. This is your inner radar being activated, snapping you out of whatever had been occupying your thinking and alerting you that someone is either addressing you or talking about something that is relevant to you.

You can capitalize on this phenomenon by letting your target audience members know right in your speech title that your presentation is designed specifically for them. The most fundamental way to do this, of course, is to highlight one or more of their pressing problems or compelling desires. Sometimes, though, you can take this a step further by creating a title that calls them by name or gives them the sense that this is what you are doing.

The most straight-forward way to do this is to insert the name of your target group into your title. If, for instance, you are a sales trainer who is looking to speak to insurance agents and investment advisors, you might give a speech entitled "How Financial Sales Professionals Can Overcome the Toughest Objections." This title leaves no doubt as to who this speech is for. Make sure, though, that your speech itself is equally well-tailored to your target audience.

Sometimes you can identify your target audience members without actually mentioning them by name. A public speaking coach, for example, could give a speech entitled "How to Click with Any Audience." While this title doesn't specifically mention who the presentation is for, it implies that it is for anyone who speaks to groups. An "audience," after all, is generally considered to be a group of people. And who would want to click with an audience? Why public speakers, of course.

A similar way to let your target audience members know that your presentation is for them is to highlight one of their common experiences or a specific problem situation they could possibly face in the future. If you are a management consultant, for instance, you might entitle a speech "How to Manage Your Team During a Crisis." Unlike a general title such as "Essential Skills for Managers," this one keys in on a specific situation (a crisis) faced by many managers. As such, it will resonate with any manager who has ever had to manage a team of people during a crisis.

Some other examples:

- How to Boost Employee Morale When Your Company is Down-sizing.
- How to Select Stocks in a Down Market
- How to Sell to People on a Budget
- Command Confidence Under Pressure
- How to Get Organized After a Move

Beckon to Beginners

How do I get started? Where do I begin? What should I do first? These are questions uppermost in the minds of those who are just entering a new field or beginning to explore a new area of interest. If your presentation focuses on addressing the questions and concerns of newcomers to your field, you need to somehow communicate this in your program title. This will let your target audience members know that your presentation is tailor-made for them.

Here are some sample speech titles that state or imply that the presentation is geared toward beginners:

- How to Break into Advertising
- The Seven Steps to Launching a Business
- How to Write Your First Book
- Getting Started in Real Estate Investing
- Fundamentals of Effective Public Speaking
- Introduction to Search Engine Optimization
- Essential People Skills for New Managers

Appeal to Advanced Audiences

How likely is it that a veteran sales professional will attend a workshop entitled "Selling 101" or "Fundamentals of Selling?" Not very. She is way past the beginning stages of her sales career. She already understands the basics. If she is going to attend a workshop on selling, it will be one that helps her build upon her solid foundation of selling skills.

So if you are a speaker who focuses on teaching advanced skills and strategies to knowledgeable audiences, take note.   Let your target audiences know, in your program title, that you will be sharing advanced or high-level information. This will hook them and make it clear that your program goes well beyond the fundamentals of your topic. At the same time, they'll have the sense that you are appealing directly to them.

Title Recipe for the Advanced Audiences

1) Create a benefit-focused title for your program.

2) Frame your solutions as being advanced with the help of such words as advanced, high-level, top, ultimate, leading edge, mastery, beyond, and breakthrough.

3) Optional: Label your intended high-level audience as such (e.g. top salespeople, experienced managers, highly skilled professionals, etc.).

To prime your thinking, here are some book titles that appeal to advanced audiences:

- Advanced Selling Strategies: The Proven System of Sales Ideas, Methods, and Techniques Used by Top Sales People Everywhere (Brian Tracy)
- The Ultimate Sales Letter (Dan Kennedy)
- Leading at a Higher Level (Ken Blanchard)
- Beyond Selling: How to Maximize Your Personal Influence (Dan Bagley III and Edward J. Reese)
- Breakthrough! How to Explode the Production of Experienced Consultants (Steven M. Finkel)

If you have studied one or more of the top people in your field and have uncovered insights into the secrets behind their success, you might also appeal to an advanced audience by highlighting this in your speech title. The true masters in any field are revered. It is natural to wonder what deep or specialized knowledge they possess. If you know, you can capitalize on this mystique by simply referring to "the masters" in your presentation title.

Here are some examples of possible speech titles that showcase the masters:

- Storytelling Techniques of Successful Speakers
- How America's Leading Companies Maintain Their Competitive Edge
- The Five Habits of Highly Prolific Writers
- Top Mental Training Strategies of Olympic Gold Medalists
- Creative Selling Techniques of Million-Dollar Sales Professionals
- How McDonald's Grew from a Hamburger Stand into a Fast Food Giant

Unlike many other effective titles, which directly promise a positive outcome or benefit, this type simply implies a positive result. The implication is that by applying what you learn in this presentation, you too can become a master and gain all of the benefits that come with that distinction.

Captivate with a Compliment

When you overhear people talking about you, it gets your attention. But if they are also complimenting or praising you, you are riveted to their words. This is really no surprise. We all crave appreciation. So why not use this to your advantage to increase the impact of your speech title? To do this, simply embed your title with a compliment or two to your target audience.

Consider, for example, this possible speech title: "How smart professionals with a successful track record become recognized thought leaders in their field." On the surface, this title simply seems to be saying the speaker will share some strategies or tactics that other professionals have used to become well-known.

On another level, however, this title conveys the idea that this program is for "smart professionals with a successful track record." If you think of yourself as someone who fits this description, you will be drawn to this program and have your ego stroked in the process.

Some other examples:

- How Gifted Students Overcome Fierce Competition to be Accepted by Top Colleges
- Success Secrets of Top Athletes who Emerge as Sports Super Stars
- How Leading Salespeople Snap Out of Slump
- How Visionary Leaders from Innovative Companies Inspire Their Teams

Chapter Four

Where's the Beef?

A once popular television commercial run by the Wendy's hamburger chain featured a little old woman who visited a variety of other restaurants in search of the perfect hamburger. Everywhere she went, she was served either a tiny hamburger on a huge bun or a burger that was composed largely of fillers. And each time, she responded with the question "Where's the beef?"

It wasn't long before this question became a popular catch phrase in American culture. Even U.S. Presidential candidate Walter Mondale posed the "Where's the beef?" question as a way of confronting his opponents' political rhetoric that was lacking in substance.

When coming across weak and ineffective speech titles, I ask a similar question: Where's the benefit?" Such titles may identify the topic of the presentation and have a certain sound of importance. But you are left guessing as to what real value this presentation may offer you or how it is relevant to your needs and wants. What is missing is the beef—the benefit.

To serve up this beef in your speech title, you need to convey how someone will profit from what they learn in your presentation. Will your insights help your listeners achieve something that they really want? Will you help them solve a pressing problem or overcome a major challenge? Somehow you need to clearly answer the question that is uppermost in the mind of any potential audience member—What's in it for me?

Some speakers try using their speech topic or subject as a title, trusting that people will just naturally translate that subject into a benefit or see it as one. But do you really want to require people to go to the effort of translating your title? People don't want to have to work to figure out how your speech will benefit them. If you don't clearly spell it out, there's a good chance that they will simply move on.

If you're a psychologist and you give your speech a topic-focused title such as "The Importance of Self-Esteem," you have not conveyed any enticing reason for someone to care about your talk. What is that "importance?" Don't keep it a mystery. Highlight it in a way that will motivate people to want to learn more.

You might, for instance, give this speech a title such as "How to Build the Self-Confidence You Need to Rise to the Top of Your Field." This talk certainly addresses the topic of self-esteem, but it also highlights a benefit that would capture the attention of anyone seeking greater professional success.

Look at the following pairs of alternative speech titles. Which title in each pair clearly has more beef?

1) Interviewing Techniques
2) Interviewing Techniques that Help You Identify Top-Level Managerial Talent

1) The Language of Sales
2) The Magic Words that Will Motivate People to Buy Whatever You are Selling

1) Staff Management
2) Bring out the Best in Your Staff

Notice the difference? In each pair above, the first title, which is topic-focused is rather abstract, static, and stuffy. In contrast, the benefit-focused alternative is specific, active, and audience-centered.

By being able to recognize the difference, you will know when, in fact, your title or subtitle communicates a clear benefit. If it does, great. If not, it's time for you to ask "Where's the beef?' Or better yet—what's the benefit?

Explore different levels of benefits

Now that you see the value of packing a benefit (or beef) into your title, you'll want to shop for the most compelling and mouth-watering benefit possible. Benefits, like beef, come in different grades. So why use a hamburger benefit when you can find one that has the allure of prime rib?

One way to identify that tasty prime rib benefit is to explore the different levels of whatever benefit readily comes to mind. Let's say that you are a leadership expert who has developed a speech with the working title "How to Be an Effective Leader." This title expresses a fairly clear, positive outcome. To uncover a benefit on a different level of abstraction, though, you can ask a couple of questions. Why is it important to be an effective leader? What will that do for your target audience member?

One answer is that it could get team members to work better together. By bringing in this higher-level outcome or result, you might refine your title to read "How to Get Your Staff Members to Work Together." With this title, you not only convey that your audience members will learn how to be more effective leaders, you are sharing a compelling positive result they can achieve by applying the leadership principles that you teach.

This simple approach of taking a benefit or outcome and asking why it is important (or what it will do for your target audience member) can be an effective way to uncover an outcome that has even more motivational power. To increase your chances of making that happen, come up with several possible answers. Then compare those answers to get a sense of which one would resonate most strongly with your target audience.

Another way to use this approach is to ask "Why is that important?" as it relates to each answer that you generate. In our example of the title "How to Be an Effective Leader," we asked why that was important and came up with the answer "to enable a leader to get team members working together." To uncover an even higher-level benefit, we could then ask why that is important.

One possible answer: If staff members are working well together, the whole team will perform at a higher level. From this, you could create the speech title "How to Create a High-Performance Team."

You now have 3 speech titles that convey different levels of benefits or outcomes: 1) How to Be an Effective Leader, 2) How to Get Your Staff Members Working Together, and 3) How to Create a High-Performance Team.

You could keep on going to generate even higher-level outcomes. It's important to realize, though, that higher isn't necessarily better. As you keep going, your outcomes will become broader and more general, your real speech topic will disappear, and you will lose the essence that is most appealing to your target audience.

Consider, for example, what would happen if you continued using this approach with the speech title "How to Create a High-Performance Team." You would ask what's important to a leader about being able to do that. One possibility is that this would enable the company or organization to become more successful.

A company owner or president would certainly see this as an exciting outcome. Other leaders within the company could also feel good about contributing to the firm's success, as it would increase their job satisfaction and position them for advancement and possible pay increases.

Yet, when you translate this outcome into a speech title, you end up with something like "How to Boost the Success and Profitability of Your Company." While this may, in fact, be the result of creating a high-performance team, this title no longer conveys anything about leadership, which is the main topic of the speech. The topic has disappeared.

Obviously, this is not what you want. At the least, you want your speech title to convey a clear sense of what your speech is really about. So when this process takes you to a point where you can no longer do that, it is time to stop. You can then look at the different titles you have generated and determine which one you feel will be most compelling to your target audience.

One of the fastest ways to grab the attention of your target audience members is to shine the spotlight on their most pressing problems or most difficult challenges.

—*Sam Wieder*

Part Two

Cooking Up Challenges

Pain is an incentive to action. Getting rid of pain is an incentive to action. Reminding people that they'll still have pain if they don't act is an incentive to action.

—*Dr. Jeffrey Lant*, Cash Copy

Chapter Five

Pour Out
Percolating Problems

A highly successful direct-response print advertisement for a first-aid remedy featured a bold, one-word headline: "Hemorrhoids?" It is easy to see why this headline was so effective. For anyone suffering with hemorrhoids, the mere mention of this affliction instantly grabbed their attention.

The writer of this ad obviously recognized the power of a headline that highlights a pressing (or in this case burning) problem. When people are struggling with a problem, they are instinctively drawn to any promise or possibility of solving it. Any mention of the problem itself is thus an emotional trigger that gets them to call up the problem state and primes them to hear about a solution.

If your speech addresses a pressing problem of your target audience, you can capitalize on this phenomenon by highlighting that problem in your title. The more clearly you can convey the essence of the problem, the better. Your objective, after all, is to get your target audience members to instantly identify with the problem and connect with the pain or challenge associated with it.

When you are developing a problem-focused speech title, there are two basic ways to approach it. You can either promise to show your target audience how to solve a problem or how to prevent one. So let's look at how you might craft a title in each of these scenarios.

Problem Resolution Titles

When you highlight a current problem of your target audience members, you can approach it in different ways. You may want to pump it up by stressing a major negative impact of the problem. You may want to create a context for the problem so that people can more readily see where it pops up. Or you may want to simply create a short, declarative statement that promises a resolution of the problem. Here are some examples of each of these different approaches:

- How to Lose Excess Pounds that Slow You Down
- How to Resolve Conflict in the Workplace
- Overcome Writer's Block

Problem Prevention Titles

Not everyone in your target audience may be currently struggling with a challenge that you address. Still, you can rein them in by showing them how to prevent the problem in the first place.

You can do this with a "problem prevention" speech title, one that gets your target audience members to focus on a potential problem that could be serious or costly. This type of title plays on their fear of damage, difficulty, or loss. You are, in effect, getting them to consider how a certain problem could hurt them, make their lives miserable, or cause them to lose something of value, such as money, time, health, energy, valuable employees, customers, or even their good looks.

Some of your target audience members may have experienced the problem in the past but never figured out how to keep it from happening again. If the problem was serious enough for them or they've encountered it repeatedly, they will be the ones to most readily respond to your appeal for problem prevention. If you frequently suffer from low back pain, for example, you would naturally perk up when reading a speech title such as "The 3 Keys to Preventing Chronic Low Back Pain."

Other members of your target audience may have never had the problem that you highlight. Still, if it is a problem that they could easily face, they should be able to see the value of avoiding it. For your problem prevention speech title to work well with this group, however, you must be able to get them to imagine the negative consequences of a potential problem and see them as a real possibility.

What is the best type of problem to highlight in a "problem prevention" speech title? At the least, it should be a problem that has serious negative consequences. Even better is a problem that your target audience members have already experienced—the more often, the better. After all, once they have felt the sting of a problem, they are primed to learn how they can prevent it from happening again.

To identify a compelling problem to highlight in your speech title, begin by asking this question: What is most important to the members of your target audience? What do they highly value? This might include such values as health, financial security, job security, freedom, reputation, professional success, family, and relationships.

The most serious problems faced by your target audience members are those that jeopardize one or more of these core values. The more importance they place on a value, the more pain they feel when it is damaged, violated, or taken away. And so naturally, they will want to do whatever they can to prevent this pain.

With this in mind, look at the top values of your target audience. Which one do you feel is their highest value related to your speech topic or area of expertise? What potential problems could violate that value? Of those problems, which one feels like it would have the most negative impact? Use this line of questioning to flush out the most compelling problem to feature in your speech title.

Let's say, for example, that you are a management consultant to the restaurant industry. Your target audience is restaurateurs who place a high value of having happy, satisfied customers. What problems could violate this value? A few possibilities might include: bad food, an unpleasant ambiance, and poor customer service.

Of these problems, you determine that poor customer service is the one that you can most effectively address in your presentation. Focusing on that, you might create a problem prevention speech title such as "Seven Steps Your Waiters Can Take to Avoid Irritating Your Customers."

Here are some other examples of problem prevention speech titles that might be used by speakers from different professions:

Profession	Problem-Prevention Title
Attorney	Avoid Costly Lawsuits
Sales Manager	Prevent Your Salespeople from Abusing Their Expense Accounts

Profession	Problem-Prevention Title
Family Counselor	Keep Your Kids Out of Trouble
Security Specialist	Prevent Burglars from Breaking into Your Business
Career Coach	Calm the Nervous Jitters that Sabotage Your Job Interviews
Nutritionist	Snacking Secrets to Prevent the Mid-day Energy Slump

What are the most pressing problems of your target audience members? What potential problems would they most want to avoid? Your answers to these questions will provide you with the starter needed to develop speech titles that harness the power of problems.

Discover what most frustrates your target audience and you'll have a key ingredient for a compelling speech title.

—Sam Wieder

Chapter Six

Fire Up Frustration

Imagine this. You're a struggling small business owner. You've tried one marketing approach after another. But nothing is really working and you can barely cover your expenses. What could you be doing wrong? How can you turn things around? What can you finally do to break free of your struggle?

What you are experiencing in this hypothetical example is pent-up frustration—something that most everyone feels from time to time. Whether you've been engaging in an ongoing battle to lose weight, get your children to behave, land a job, find an ideal mate, or achieve that goal that has always seemed to be just out of reach, you know what it feels like to be frustrated. And if given the chance, you'd do whatever you could to free yourself of that feeling.

That may also be the mindset and emotional state of your target audience members. In fact, they may very well be feeling a frustration that you can help them resolve with your presentation. If that's the case, you owe it to yourself and to them to identify what it is. Even better, if you can create a speech title that somehow conveys that frustration and/or offers a promise to resolve it, you will have a powerful means of attracting people to your program.

How do you do this? Through the use of words and phrases that are associated with either frustration or the relief of overcoming frustration. Below is a listing of common frustration-related words and phrases, divided into five categories. Use this as a basic ingredient list that you can draw from in whipping up a speech title that taps into the frustrations of your target audience.

Of course, this might also inspire you to come up with similar words and phrases. If you do that, however, I suggest that you keep your language clean so as not to offend the more sensitive members of your target audience.

Frustration Ingredient List

Core Descriptive Words: frustrate, struggle, battle, endure, exasperate, desperate, blocked

Frustration Pumps (Words that pump up the level of frustration in a sentence when placed in front of such words as "struggle" or "battle"): ongoing, continuous, perpetual, endless, never-ending

Pump-up words especially useful in questions that evoke frustration:

1) Still (Are you *still* struggling?)
2) Ever (Will you *ever* figure it out?)

Frustration Phrases

Pushed to the limit
Can't take it any more/any longer
The last straw
Enough already!
Enough is enough!
All you can stand
Not again!
Oy Vey!

Words and Phrases for Resolving Frustration: break free, breakthrough, bust loose, escape, turn around, rise above, get past, surmount, overcome, win, resolve, conquer

Frustration Relief

Finally!
At last!
At long last!
Once and for all!

Want to see some of these words and phrases in action? Here is a sampling of book titles that harness the power of frustration.

But I Might Need It Someday!
How to organize your life and win the clutter battle once and for all (by Patty Kreamer, Professional Organizer)

Stop the Insanity!
Change the way you look and feel—forever
(New York Times best-seller by Susan Powter)

Enough is enough!
Stop enduring and start living your extraordinary life
(by Jane Straus)

I Know My Child Can Do Better!
A Frustrated Parent's Guide to Educational Options
(by Anne Hearon Rambo)

Breakthrough!
Proven Strategies to Overcome Creative Block and Spark Your Imagination (by Alex Cornell)

Now that you have a basic ingredient list and some sample titles to prime your thinking, here is a simple recipe you can follow to cook up your own frustration-based speech title.

Recipe for a Frustration-Based Speech Title

1) Identify a common frustration of your target audience, one that you address in your presentation.

2) Create a speech title and/or subtitle that conveys the above frustration and promises to resolve it.

3) Option: Use an expression of frustration as your speech title and a statement promising to resolve that frustration as your subtitle.

Chapter Seven

Time to Get Cooking: How to Create Urgency

If you are lazing around in your easy chair on a relaxing Saturday morning, you might ponder the possibility of stepping outside at some point to get some fresh air and sunshine. If you suddenly discover, however, that your house is on fire, there's no pondering. You are high-tailing it out of there pronto.

By the same token, if you want to get the members of your target audience high-tailing it to your presentation, you may want to light a fire under them, so to speak. Your program title may highlight a solid benefit or two that would interest people in your presentation. But what would compel them to want to attend your program now?

Your target audience members may have busy lives, with many other things competing for their time and attention. Or maybe they are attending a conference where there are a few other break-out sessions being held at the same time as yours. Why should they make attending your program a priority?

Conference and event planners consider many proposals when booking speakers for their upcoming events. Why should they choose you over other speakers? And why should they book you as soon as possible rather than waiting a year?

To help prompt immediate action, bring a sense of urgency into your speech title. Give people a reason to act now. Just as a milk carton is stamped with an expiration date, you can stamp your speech title with the sense that your information is best if used as soon as possible.

To create a sense of urgency, you want your speech title to convey at least one of the following messages:

- Act now or lose
- Act now or a problem will get worse
- Act now and win
- Now is an especially good time to act (and benefit from what you have to share)

The desires to avoid pain or prevent loss are especially powerful motivators, playing a role in most every motivational message. Even if your message focuses on what people can gain from your presentation, you are implying that they will lose in some way if they pass up the opportunity to attend your program.

Speech Title Models that Convey Urgency

Model #1: Act Now or Lose

Specialize or Starve:
How to Capture a Market Niche that will Help Your Business Survive and Thrive in Today's Economy

Legal Documents You Need Now to Safeguard Your Assets and Be Ready for the Unexpected

How to Reduce the Financial Bite of the Coming Tax Hike

Model #2: Act Now or a Problem Will Get Worse

How to Curb Your Growing Credit Card Debt Before It Spirals Out of Control

How to Keep Small Disagreements from Destroying Your Relationships

What's Eating You?
How Your Fast Food Diet May be Steadily Gnawing Away at Your Health

Model #3: Act Now and Win

Jumpstart Your Business:
How to Prepare Now for Record Sales in the Coming Year

Secure Your Financial Future Today:
Five Steps You Must Take Now to Guarantee a Secure Retirement

How to Command Confidence and Be at Your Best on Your Next Big Job Interview

Model #4: Now is an especially good time to act.

How to Boost Your Sales to Today's Top Growth Industry

Gain the Edge:
Be Among the First to Capitalize on the Housing Recovery

Essential Selling Skills You Need Now More Than Ever

Ready to create your own compelling speech title that spurs people to drop what they are doing and sign up for your program now? Here's the recipe.

Recipe for a Speech Title the Conveys Urgency

1) Create a benefit or outcome-focused speech title.

2) Add a sense of urgency to your title using one or more of the four basic motivational models.

3) If you are using a title/subtitle combination and one of them is loss-focused, it is generally a good idea to make the other one outcome-focused.

4) Generate several possible titles using the above recipe and select the one that you feel will have the most impact with your target audience.

Part Three

Serving Up Structure

The more you say, the less people remember.
The fewer the words, the greater the profit.

—*Francois de Salignac Fenelon*

Chapter Eight

Make Your Title Short and Sweet

I once walked into a busy Italian deli that was lined with display cases of meats, cheeses, breads, nuts, prepared foods and baked goods. As I walked through the store, I was naturally drawn to different "free sample" stations. At one station, I sampled a small cube of delicious imported cheese. At another, I was given a small paper cup of warm bread pudding that melted in my mouth.

While most everything in the store looked tempting, it was the foods that I was able to sample that really engaged my senses and primed me to want more. One tasty bite of a food was all it took for me to know if it was for me.

Likewise, when you are developing a main title for your next presentation, you would do well to compress it into a short and sweet sound bite. The fewer words you can use, the better. After all, the shorter your title, the faster and easier it will be for people to digest your words. Of course, at the same time, you need to make sure that the words you choose offer a savory taste of what you have to offer.

There are different ways of structuring a short, pithy title that will whet people's appetite for the wisdom you have to share in your speech or seminar. So let's look at some of the most compelling possibilities.

Profit from the Power Pair

What is a Power Pair you may wonder? It is a phrase I coined to describe a simple but powerful form for an effective speech title. In fact, the phrase "power pair" is actually an example of the form itself.

Quite simply, a Power Pair is a title that combines two words that work together to powerfully communicate the essence of your speech topic. You might use a Power Pair to convey the major outcome that your speech is designed to help your audience members to achieve, such as "financial fitness" or "optimal health." You might also use a Power Pair to express your particular slant or approach to your subject, such as "outside-the-box marketing," "spiritual healing," or "conversational coaching."

While a Power Pair can concisely convey the essence of your topic to grab people's attention, you will generally need to add a subtitle to more clearly and completely spell out how someone will benefit from attending your presentation. This is especially important with Power Pair titles that don't communicate a clear benefit, such as with the title "Innovative Leadership."

If you can create a Power Pair in which both words start with the same letter or sound, that will help pump it up with the power of alliteration. If you can't do this, however, that is also fine. What is most important is that your words meld to illuminate the core concept of your speech. If you can make that happen, your title will ring loud and true, whether or not your words alliterate.

Ready to craft a Power Pair that you might use as your speech title? Here's how to start. Just ask yourself how you might accurately describe your speech topic in only two words. Or if you could sum up in two words a positive outcome that your speech will help people to achieve, what would those two words be? Generate several possibilities and see what works best.

Try a Triple

Sometimes the two concept words you want to convey in your title don't quite function as you would like when you simply try to slam them together. Maybe they don't naturally meld into a single concept. Or maybe these two core words would work better together if you separated them and connected them with a single word that establishes the relationship between them. If that's the case, a three-word title (or a "triple") can be even more effective than a Power Pair.

One especially powerful form of the Triple employs the preposition "with" as the connector word. Start by identifying the main skill or outcome you address in your talk. Then, come up with a word or concept that adds an intriguing dimension of meaning. Place the preposition "with" between these two words and voila—you've got your speech title.

Some examples:

- Speak with Impact
- Persuade with Power
- Excel with Ease
- Lead with Heart

Another useful form of the Triple uses the connector "without" to show your target audience members that you can help them remove the pain, struggle, danger, or unpleasantness from achieving something that they want. This, in fact, was the approach used by financial expert Charles Givens with his book title "Wealth without Risk."

If you can create a Triple with only three words, great. But if you need to add another word to describe one of your core concepts, this is also fine, since the triple in this form refers to two concepts and one connector. Even with four words, your title is still crisp and concise.

A few examples of a Triple featuring "without:"

- Weight Loss without Dieting
- Prospecting without Cold Calls
- Dating without Pressure

You can also create Triples by placing a variety of other prepositions between your two core concept words. These valuable and useful connectors could include: of, at, by, in, to, toward, from, for, before, during, after, across, over, around, between, through, beyond, under, and above.

Here are some examples of prepositions in action:

- Working by Referral
- Triumph over Tragedy
- Exercise during Pregnancy
- Managing through Uncertainty
- Stress Management for Accountants
- Playing to Win

You can create a Triple that appeals directly to your target audience by making the possessive pronoun "your" the central word in your title. This can help to grab people's attention and get them to relate to your topic.

A few examples of this approach:

- Building Your Business
- Mastering Your Money
- Developing Your Vocabulary

Call People to Action

A short, inspiring call to action can attract attention while getting your target audience members to focus on something they want to be able to do. With this type of title, you are framing this outcome or ability in the form of a command. For maximum effect, make this command clear, concise and vigorous. If you want, you could place the words "How to" in front of this title and that would also work. But if you want to be more crisp and concise, a simple call-to-action format will certainly do the job.

Some examples:

- Take the Lead
- Make Things Happen
- Power Up Your Presentations
- Ignite Your Energy
- Focus on What Counts

Double Up Your Action Call

To beef up your title and still keep it concise, you could combine a pair of two-word calls to action, separated by a comma. This, in fact, was exactly the approach that writing expert Robert Bly used with his book title "Write More, Sell More." In this case, Bly repeats the second word "more," which enhances the sound and the rhythm of the title. Repeating the introductory verb in two parallel phrases, author Joe Henderson also harnesses the power of repetition in his book title "Run Farther, Run Faster."

This title form can also be also be used to imply a relationship between the two calls to action. If, for example, you were giving a productivity workshop for writers, you might call it "Procrastinate Less, Write More." In a similar vein, an investment advisor might pack two related bits of investment advice into a presentation entitled "Buy Low, Sell High."

Go from Action Call to Result

One way to better bring out the benefit in an action call title is to follow your call to action with a compelling benefit of taking the action. To make this type of title as powerful as possible, it is also useful to express both the action call and the result in as few words as possible. Ideally, you might shoot for a 1-2 word action call and a 1-3 word result.

Typically, the way to connect an action with a result linguistically is with a preposition such as "to." (e.g. Eat a variety of fresh vegetables to stay healthy.) With shorter sentences and phrases, however, the conjunction "and" is often used, with even greater effect.

One notable example of this is the title of Napoleon Hill's classic self-help book "Think and Grow Rich." In this case, Hill implores you to "think" (his call to action) to set in motion the forces that will enable you to "get rich" (the positive result).

Some other examples:

- Speak Up and Win
- Walk and Get Fit
- Laugh and Get Healthy
- Invest Now and Retire Secure

In the next chapter, we will take a deeper look at how to combine two core concepts into a single title. As a warm-up for that chapter, you might want to generate a couple of four-word "call-to-action" titles for your speech topic using this double-up formula. This will give you great practice in boiling your topic down to its essence. And as a bonus, you just might end up creating a crisp, concise, and high-impact title for your presentation.

Double your pleasure, double your fun, with Double Mint, Double Mint, Double Mint Gum.

—*Popular Wrigley's advertising jingle*

Chapter Nine

Try a Double Shot
Of Expressiveness

Many speech titles highlight only one major problem, benefit, or outcome. Often, though, you can boost the impact of your title by also introducing a second concept. Here are some different ways you can do this.

Double Your Pleasure

You can double the allure of your presentation with a title that incorporates two related or complementary benefits or positive outcomes. As you go beyond two benefits, your target audience's ability to mentally process your positives will generally start to diminish. But only two positive outcomes can usually be grasped by almost anyone.

Some examples of double benefit titles:

- How to Build Your Network and Boost Your Sales
- Boost Your Confidence and Land Your Dream Job
- Gain Financial Security and Enjoy Your Retirement
- How Win Friends and Influence People (a classic self-improvement book by Dale Carnegie)

Separate the Benefits

When your presentation teaches people how to do something, there are two main inherent benefits in what you have to offer. One is the benefit of learning how to do something. The other is the benefit that your audience members will enjoy by applying the process or skill that you have taught them.

A voice coach, for example, might develop a speech title such as "How to Develop a Commanding Voice." This title promises two benefits: 1) an understanding of the process of developing your voice and 2) a commanding voice, if you follow the process. With this title, the two benefits are combined into one tight package.

Just as some cooking recipes may call for you to separate an egg (i.e. remove the yolk from the white), you may want to separate the two benefits in the type of title above to create a more tasty and potent result. By doing this, you could transform the above title into: "How to Develop a Voice that Commands Attention."

By structuring your title in this way, you showcase the positive result. You're not tucking it in behind the word "voice." You are ending with it. This leaves your reader clearly focused on the ultimate positive outcome.

Some other examples of this format:

- Design a Diet that Unleashes Your Energy
- How to Write a Book that Gives You Expert Status
- How to Develop an Investment Portfolio that Secures Your Financial Future

Show the Benefit, Add a Qualifier

Another way to bring double power to your speech title is to open with a positive outcome and then follow it up with a qualifier that addresses a potential concern about your claim. This can excite your target audience members about what you have to offer and then immediately show them that your approach is an especially good fit for them.

Some examples of using a qualifying phrase to power up a speech title:

- Lose Excess Weight Without Giving Up the Foods You Love
- Get the Best Night's Sleep of Your Life Without Taking Sleeping Pills or Buying a New Mattress
- How to Attract a Flood of New Clients—Even If You Hate Sales and Marketing

Get the idea? You simply take a compelling outcome and amplify it with a qualifying phrase that quiets people's concerns about your approach.

Solve the Problem, Show the Result

Yet another way to give your title a double shot is to open with a problem resolution statement and follow it with the resulting positive outcome. In this way, you get people's attention with a promise to help them address a major problem and then excite them about what is possible when the problem has been resolved.

Some examples of the "problem resolution" double:

- How to Stop Worrying and Start Living (a book by self-improvement legend Dale Carnegie)
- Slash Expenses and Boost Your Profitability
- How to Handle the Toughest Objections and Double Your Sales Closing Ratio

Contrast Before and After

The "before and after" double shot promises to move someone from a situation of struggle or failure to a state of ease or success.

Some examples:

- How to Build a Fledgling Business into a Million-Dollar Operation
- How to Go from Stuck to Unstoppable
- How to Turn Struggling Students into Star Learners

Dish Out a Double Negative

As a rule, it is a good idea to include at least one compelling positive outcome in your speech title and/or subtitle. Sometimes, though, it may be more effective to simply focus on two negatives—a problem or problem resolution statement and the negative result that could happen if the problem isn't resolved. This effectively enables you to pump up the pain that your target audience wants to avoid. So in situations where you feel that pain may be a better motivator than gain or pleasure, this may be the way to go.

Some examples of "double negative" speech titles:

- Interviewing Mistakes that Will Cost You the Job
- Stop Eating Problem Foods that Cause Your Weight to Skyrocket
- Stop Worrying Before You Make Yourself Sick
- Snap Out of Your Depression Before Your Life Implodes

Numbers and measures, by their very nature, convey a sense of value. Bring the right number or two into any speech title and you can instantly double or triple the perceived value of your presentation.

—*Sam Wieder*

Chapter Ten

Add a Measure of Value

Something magical can happen when you introduce numbers into your language. What was general becomes specific. What was vague becomes clear. What was abstract becomes real.

As a speaker, you can harness this magical power in crafting your speech title, not to perform a mere parlor trick, but to attract the attention and spark the curiosity of your target audience.

Your ideal audience members are either struggling with a challenge that you can help them address or they are in need of your guidance to achieve something that they really want. Most often, though, they don't know why they are struggling or what they need to do to move more easily toward their goals. That's why they need to attend your presentation and hear your message.

Of course, to effectively attract people to your program, you need to convince your target audience members that you understand the challenges that have mystified them or know the concrete steps they need to take to achieve what they want. One powerful way to do this is to quantify the challenges they face or the major steps that will move them forward. Bring a number into your title and you suddenly create the sense that you are an expert who offers solid insights and real solutions. So, let's look at different ways that you can do this.

Point to the Underlying Reasons

The most effective speech titles and/or subtitles typically provide a clear, specific, and compelling reason for someone to attend the presentation. One possible way to make your title even more appealing to your target audience is to spark their curiosity about what they don't know. To do this, you might point to the reasons behind the problem or outcome that is the focus of your title.

A chiropractor, for example, might entitle her speech "The 5 Reasons that Office Workers Experience Chronic Low Back Pain." This title not only conveys a clear problem, but makes you curious about what may be causing it. What's more, the mention of 5 different causes boosts your curiosity even more.

An investment advisor might give a speech entitled "The 3 Main Investment Strategies that Have Enabled Warren Buffet to Become One of the World's Richest Men." Here the investment strategies are the reasons behind the highlighted outcome of amassing great wealth.

Best-selling author Steven Covey also used this approach in titling his book "The Seven Habits of Highly Effective People." In this case, of course, the seven habits are the reasons.

Whether you use the word "reasons" in your title or refer to a specific kind of reason (such as a strategy or habit), the effect is the same. You arouse people's curiosity about the underlying causes of a problem or the key factors that can help them to achieve something they want.

Showcase mistakes

Mistakes—we all make them. Sometimes they're obvious. Other times they're not. What can really be frustrating is when you are struggling to do something because you are making mistakes that you're not even aware of. When this happens, you wonder "What could I be doing wrong?"

As a speaker, you can tap into the mystery within this question and use it to create a speech title that evokes curiosity and interest. You do this by shining the spotlight on the most likely mistakes of your audience members.

Two examples:

- The Five Biggest Mistakes that Prevent Financial Advisors from Attracting Clients
- The Seven Mistakes that Cause Restaurants to Lose Customers

These two examples highlight the two different ways to craft a "mistakes" title. The first connects mistakes to the target audience members' struggle to achieve something that they want. The second links mistakes to a problem they would like to avoid or keep from happening again.

Whether your speech title is outcome-focused or problem-focused, you can bring in the element of mistakes to spice it up. In either case, you leave people wondering if perhaps they may be unknowingly making some of the mistakes you will discuss. In addition, the assumption built into this type of title is that once you have pointed out the mistakes, you will then share the right things to do.

Step up your speech title

Often when people attend a speech, workshop, or teleclass, they don't simply want to hear general information about a topic. They want to learn the steps they can take to achieve what they want. Knowing this, you can often command greater attention by using your title to broadcast the fact that you will be sharing a specific, step-by-step process.

Some examples of a process-focused title:

- The Seven Steps to Landing Your Dream Job
- The Five Steps to Handling Difficult Customers
- The 6-Step Process for Breaking the Procrastination Habit Once and For All

Get the idea? You're not just promising to share some helpful ideas. You're highlighting a concrete process that offers people specific guidance and direction.

How to Pick the Winning Number

Since numbers are often seen as measures of value, they can make your speech content appear to be valuable, especially when you introduce a number of 3 or higher. Of course, you must exercise some discretion in deciding how many significant points you want to make in your speech and announce in your title.

If you are giving a one-hour speech that is billed as offering "21 Ideas for Business Success," you are signaling the fact that most likely you won't be covering any one idea in any great depth. There just isn't time. As a result, your potential audience members may get the impression that your speech will contain very little of the specific, how-to information that they crave. So rather than trying to cover 21 ideas, you may be able to convey more real value by announcing that you will be discussing just a handful.

Some audiences, however, may get excited at the prospect of hearing a cornucopia of ideas. So you really need to determine if your audience falls into this category.

What is the ideal number of points to highlight in this type of title? That depends. You first want to consider how many points you feel you can effectively make, given the time frame of your presentation. Just doing that may give you a fairly good idea of what would work well.

If your speech title focuses on reasons or mistakes, you could probably address as many as 9 or 10 in a one-hour presentation. That's because you can generally make these types of points without too much in-depth discussion. Also, when you highlight reasons or mistakes in your speech title, you are not really evoking the expectation that you will be presenting a lot of specific, how-to information.

When, on the other hand, your speech title and your speech focus on tactics, strategies, methods, processes, or approaches, this is exactly what you are doing. You are clearly saying that you have some meaty, how-to ideas to share. When this is the case, you most likely would do well to limit yourself to from 3 to 6 major points for a one-hour presentation. Again, though, base your final determination of how many major ideas you feel you can effectively cover in the time allotted.

As a rule, people won't care a lick about the methods you use in your business or profession until they recognize that you can solve their particular problems.

—Sam Wieder

Chapter Eleven

How and When to Mix in Your Method

Most effective speech titles, as a rule, focus on either a pressing problem or a desired outcome. If you can avoid mentioning your method or approach for helping people overcome the problem or achieve the outcome, this is typically the best way to go. After all, people will generally be much more interested in how they will profit from your talk than in your particular method or approach.

Consider, for example, these two possible speech titles:

- The Johnson Income Tax Preparation Method
- How to Increase Your Income Tax Deductions by 20-40%

The first title leaves you thinking, "Hmm, I wonder what that's about. Sounds like it would be about as exciting as watching paint dry." The second one, on the other hand, is likely to have you respond with, "Wow, that's for me! I'd love to learn how I can pay lower taxes."

The above titles could, of course, be combined into the title "How to Increase Your Income Tax Deductions by 20-40% with the Johnson Income Tax Preparation Method. But unless the Johnson Method is already widely known, tacking it on to the title adds little or nothing of real value.

It simply weighs down the title and detracts from the benefit-focused message.

There is, however, a situation in which your method may serve a useful purpose in your title. Sometimes, your method or approach may be a defining element in your speech topic. When this is the case, you will want to bring in and even showcase your method in your speech title.

One speech title I've used in the past, for example, is "How to Attract Clients through Public Speaking." If I sliced my method (public speaking) from this title, I would simply be left with "How to Attract Clients." While this title is certainly benefit-focused and of potential interest to any professional in need of clients, it doesn't appeal to the specific audience I want to target.

Nor is my talk right for just anyone. Many professionals have absolutely no interest in speaking to groups. Some will even shake in their shoes at the thought of doing so. They are not the people I want to attract.

Since public speaking is a defining element of my topic, I need to refer to it in some way in my speech title. This will grab the attention of those who are interested in using public speaking as a marketing method and let everyone else know that this just isn't the program for them.

The preposition I used to connect my main benefit (attracting clients) with my method (public speaking) was "through" (although in some cases the word "by" works a little better as a connector). So if I had to summarize this as a formula, it would be: "How to X (achieve a benefit) through/by Y (method). And to further clarify this formula, the method is not the formal name of a method, such as the Hammerblatt Approach. It is a word or phrase that conveys a concept that most anyone would understand (such as public speaking).

Some more examples:

- How to Find Job Opportunities in Your Field through Online Searches
- How to Locate Joint Venture Partners through Social Media
- How to Identify the Most Profitable Investments by Crunching the Right Numbers

The above sample titles begin with the benefit or positive outcome and end with a method that is a defining element of the speech topic. Another way to structure these titles is to reverse the order by beginning with the method and ending with the positive outcome. To establish the proper relationship between the major components of this re-structured title, you would simply replace the propositions "through" or "by" with "to."

These re-structured titles, then, would be written as follows:

- How to Use Online Searches to Find Job Opportunities in Your Field
- How to Use Social Media to Locate Joint Venture Partners
- Crunch the Right Numbers to Identify the Most Profitable Investment Opportunities

Which works better—placing the positive result first or second? I really think that this is a judgment call.

Conventional copywriting wisdom suggests that you should generally lead with the benefit. Sometimes, though, that can result in a speech title that sounds somewhat awkward and doesn't have quite the impact of one that places the benefit at the end.

Consider, for example, the following two alternative titles for the same speech:

- How to Improve Your Vision through Simple Eye Exercises
- How to Use Simple Eye Exercises to Improve Your Vision

Both titles convey the same basic message. My preference, though, is for the second title, as it seems to embody a much greater sense of rhythm and flow. What's more, the second title leaves you thinking about the benefit of improving your vision rather than wondering what those mysterious eye exercises could be.

In other situations, though, I just might want to lead with the benefit. Consider, for example, these two alternative titles for the same speech:

- How to Attract Clients through Public Speaking
- How to Use Public Speaking to Attract Clients

Here, I actually prefer the first title, which leads with the benefit and uses the preposition "through" to point to the method. To my ear, the first title simply flows and functions better than the second. I'm fine with ending my title with my method—public speaking—since this is something of interest to my target audience. So in essence, this title is telling them that they can achieve something that they want (attracting clients) by doing something that they already like or love (speaking to groups). How great is that?

The second title, on the other hand, puts forth the concept of how to "use" public speaking to attract clients. While this may be a grammatically acceptable way of conveying this idea, it doesn't quite set right with me. Through the word "use" in this instance, it sounds, in a subtle way, like I am offering a method of manipulating people to want to do business with you. This, in fact, is the exact opposite of what I teach.

My focus is on showing professionals how they can inspire members of their target audience to want to work with them. Not to "use" public speaking as a device to corral new clients but rather to naturally attract ideal clients through the process of giving a winning presentation.

I realize, of course, that I am making some fine distinctions here. But that is what you must also do in choosing the right words and crafting a title that will put your speech in just the right light.

This is why it is often helpful to consider at least a couple of different ways of structuring your speech title. If one title doesn't look, sound, or feel quite right, you have something to compare it with in your efforts to find a title that hits the mark.

Think left and think right and think low and think high.
Oh the thinks you can think up if only you try.

—*Dr. Seuss*

Part Four

Advanced Recipes for Creative Cooking

Using a metaphorical approach to introduce your idea
helps people to see it fresh, as if for the first time.

—*Sam Horn*, Pop!

Chapter Twelve

Munch on the Magic
Of Metaphor

One powerful way to engage people's interest is through the use of a metaphor—a figure of speech in which one thing is suggested as being representative or symbolic of something else. It is the merging of two worlds of meaning that can enable people to more quickly and deeply grasp your message.

Jack Canfield and Mark Victor Hansen capitalized on the magic of metaphor with their best-selling book Chicken Soup for the Soul. Just as chicken soup is thought to have healing and restorative effects on the human body, their book was designed to have a similar impact on the human spirit. Consisting of a collection of real-life inspirational stories, the book truly offered nourishment for the soul.

This title metaphor worked so well, in fact, that they went on to publish a whole series of "Chicken Soup" books targeted to a wide variety of markets. You might say that they rode that train all the way to the bank, which, in case you didn't notice, is itself a metaphor.

Another author who hit it big with a metaphor title was John Gray, with his best-selling book "Men are from Mars, Women are from Venus." He wasn't, of course, claiming that men and women actually come from different planets. Just that it often seems that way based on how differently they think and communicate. In any event, both men and women snatched up the book to learn how they could break through the interplanetary communication barrier.

Perhaps one of the most prolific users of metaphor titles is best-selling business book author Harvey Mackay. He first struck gold with his New York Times best-seller "How to Swim with the Sharks without being Eaten Alive." Contrary to how it might sound, this wasn't a book about how to go snorkeling in a shark-infested part of the ocean. Rather, this was a book about how to survive in the dangerous waters of business where hungry competitors are lurking.

A master networker, Mackay also wrote a book entitled "Dig Your Well Before You're Thirsty," which he subtitled "The Only Networking Book You'll Ever Need." In relation to networking, his "dig your well" metaphor conveyed the idea that you should develop strong relationships with people before you need to call upon them for help. Of course, to make this connection to networking, you really needed to read his subtitle.

This offers a valuable lesson for speakers. In a speech title, a metaphor can be a great attention-grabbing vehicle that powerfully communicates a sage piece of wisdom or advice. But to make it clear and relevant to your target audience, you'll often need to spell out its meaning in your subtitle.

Ideally, in order to make your explanation as easy as possible, you'll want to begin by choosing a metaphor that is the best possible fit for the point you want to make.

One especially effective metaphor that is often used in the realm of business networking is the concept of "planning seeds" or "sowing and reaping." What makes this such as fitting metaphor is that it contains multiple levels of symbolism.

Consider the many different ways that farming (or seed planting) and networking are alike:

- Both require some initial preparation; farming—plowing the field; networking—uncovering a fertile environment to make profitable contacts.
- Both include an initiation process that involves taking many repetitive actions: farming—planting many seeds; networking—meeting many people.
- Both involve a cultivation process: farming—watering the seeds and tending to the crops as they grow: networking—nurturing and building relationships.
- Both can result in a rich harvest: farming—an abundant crop; networking—the support and opportunities that come from strong, well-cultivated relationships.

With "sowing and reaping" used as a metaphor for networking, you are able to easily grasp all of these similarities, even without them being elaborated. What's more, you are left with a deeper understanding of the whole process of networking.

In contrast, this isn't so much the case with Harvey Mackay's title metaphor "Dig Your Well Before You're Thirsty." Yes, in the context of networking, this title can help make the point that you should build relationships with people before you need to call upon them for help. And certainly the act of drawing water from a well could be likened to drawing help and support from the people in your network.

But digging a single well is not really symbolic of the process of networking, which involves initiating and cultivating relationships with many people. I'm sure that Mackay realized this. My hunch is that he went with the "well" metaphor mainly to distinguish himself from the many other networking experts who had made the "sowing and reaping" metaphor so commonplace.

This shows that for a metaphor to work in a book or speech title, it doesn't need to be perfectly symbolic of your topic or be an ideal match on multiple levels of meaning. Naturally, it will be more powerful if it is. What's most important, though, is for your metaphor to clearly convey the main point you want to make.

Finding the Right Metaphor

To find an appropriate metaphor for your speech title, begin my taking a deep breath and letting it out slowly. (Not quite the first step you expected, was it?) This will get some oxygen to your brain and enable you to more easily make metaphorical connections. Or as you might say—to prime your mental pump.

Now that your mind is starting to clear, ask yourself these two key questions:

1) What is a defining element of your speech topic?
2) In what other realm of experience does this element play a prominent role?

I realize, of course, that right about now these questions have your eyes spinning around inside your head. So let me give you an example to clarify this.

Let's say that you are giving a speech on self-motivation. A defining element of this topic is getting yourself moving toward your goals. To find an appropriate metaphor for this, ask yourself this: What other realm of experience also involves getting yourself moving?"

One possibility might be driving a car. When you think of getting a car moving, one phrase that might come to mind is "starting your engine." Others might include: "put your foot on the gas pedal" or "shift into drive." These are all phrases that you can use to make driving a metaphor for self-motivation.

Drawing on these different aspects of your metaphor, you might create such speech titles as:

- How to Fire Up Your Engine to Get Your Next Big Project Off to a Fast Start
- Strategies to Help You Put on the Gas When You Feel Yourself Coasting
- How to Shift into Drive When You Feel Stuck in Neutral

Another possible metaphor to use for a talk on self-motivation might be walking. Here you could use such metaphorical phrases as "taking the first step," "picking up the pace," or "tripping over your own feet."

Get the idea? You're simply taking common descriptive phrases from another realm of experience and bringing them into play in your speech title. To come up with the best possible metaphor to use in your speech title, you may want to use this whole process with a few different realms of experience. This will give you some basis for comparison to determine what seems to work best.

Once you come up with a suitable metaphorical realm, it is amazing how easily the perfect words and phrases from that realm will bubble up in your mind if you just relax enough to let that happen. If this isn't happening, that's generally a good sign that the metaphor you've chosen isn't the best fit for your purposes.

That's fine. Just move on to another possibility. One key to finding effective metaphors and mining them for their descriptive gold is to approach the whole process with a sense of playfulness. In short, have some fun with this!

To further prime your thinking, here are some other examples of possible speech titles that capture the magic of metaphor:

- Ride the Wave of the Next Hottest Trend in the Food Service Industry
- How to Play to Win in the Game of Business
- Dance Your Way through Difficult Negotiations
- Breathe New Life into Your Marriage
- How to Maintain Your Financial Footing when the Market is in a Free Fall

To build your metaphor muscles, see what descriptive words or phrases come to mind for each of the following topic/metaphor combinations:

Topic	Metaphor
Arguments	Sparring/Boxing
Networking	Dating
Writing	Cooking
Eating	Fueling your car
Investing	Gardening
Selling	Baseball

Chapter Thirteen

Savor the Flavor
of Fairy Tales

Children's literature provides a rich source of ready-made metaphors that can be employed in a speech title. Especially useful are well-known fairy tales and children's stories. After all, by referring to a familiar story, you can quickly capture people's attention and create a framework of understanding for your message.

One speaker who made great use of fairy tales and children's stories in his speech titles was Mick Biancheria, a former competitor in the Toastmasters International Speech Contest. One of his signature contest-winning speeches was called the Pinnochio Syndrome, a talk about the importance of honesty in life. As honesty is a central theme in the story of Pinnochio, he was able to refer to different elements of the story to make and anchor the major points of his speech.

Biancheria opened his speech with the line "If you lie, your nose will grow." That was all that his audience members needed to hear to be transported back to their childhood memories of this fabled story of a puppet that was transformed into a real boy. Having instantly captured everyone's attention and imagination, he was then able to bring to light the story's deeper meaning.

You too can use this approach by developing a speech title that highlights a well-known fairy tale or other story from popular culture. For this approach to work for you, of course, you must be able to find a popular story that you can easily relate to your speech topic. If you find one that is a good match, though, you are ready to play with this. Just hook people with a reference to a popular story in your title and then relate it to your topic in a benefit-focused subtitle.

To prime your thinking, here are some examples of possible speech titles that highlight references to familiar stories or popular culture.

- Where was Humpty Dumpty's Chiropractor?
  How Chiropractic can Speed Your Recovery after a Fall
- Embracing the Spirit of the Three Musketeers:
  How to Get Your Team Working Together—One for All and All for One
- Reviving Romeo and Juliet:
  How to Bring Your Romance Back to Life
- Lessons from Rip Van Winkle:
  How to Finally Get a Good Night's Sleep
- Standing Up to Frankenstein:
  How to Deal with Monstrous Behavior

Chapter Fourteen

Use a Catch Phrase: The Fast Food of Titles

Even the best cooks will sometimes turn to instant soup or pre-packaged dinners when they are pressed for time and want a meal that is quick and easy. As a speech title chef, you too may want to consider something similar. In your case, though, your instant, ready-made option is a catch phrase—a catchy, often-repeated sentence or phrase drawn from popular culture.

Advertisers seek to create catch phrases they can use as memorable slogans for their products or services. Other catch phrases will emerge from television shows and popular movies. When a sentence or phrase reaches "catch phrase" status, it can be marketing gold. Like a wild fire that rages through a dry forest, a catch phrase can sweep through the consciousness and language of the masses.

You, in turn, may be able to piggyback on the popularity of a catch phrase by putting it to work as a presentation title. This is simply a matter of finding a catch phrase that is highly relevant to your presentation topic and then combining it with a subtitle that conveys that relevance and highlights a benefit to your target audience. In this combination, the catch phrase will grab people's attention, while your subtitle will provide a clear, compelling reason for them to attend your presentation.

To prime your thinking, here are some examples of catch phrases that might be used as speech titles, along with possible subtitles that might be added to clarify the topic and drive home the value of the presentation.

"Can you hear me now?"
(From a Verizon Wireless television ad)

- How to Speak so That People Will Listen
- How to Make Sure that Your Marketing Message is Heard in a Crowded Marketplace

"Is That Your Final Answer?"
(From the Game Show "Who Wants to Be a Millionaire?")

- How to Overcome the Toughest Objections
- How to Get Real Help from Customer Service Professionals

"Make Him an Offer He Can't Refuse"
(From the 1972 movie "The Godfather")

- How to Create an Irresistible Offer for Whatever You Are Selling
- Insider Secrets to Being a Master Negotiator

"Live Long and Prosper"
(From the 1960's television series "Star Trek")

- How to Plan for a Financially Secure Retirement
- Longevity Secrets of the World's Oldest People

"May the Force Be With You"
(From the 1977 movie "Star Wars")

- How to Maintain Vibrant Energy in Today's Toxic World
- How to Stay Confident Under Pressure

"Take Me to Your Leader"
(From the 1953 cartoon "Extraterrestrial Aliens")

- How Top Sales Pro's Get Past the Gate Keeper
- How to Find the Ultimate Decision Maker in Any Sales Situation

Frisbeetarianism is the belief that when you die, your soul
goes up on the roof and gets stuck.

—George Carlin

Chapter Fifteen

Create Curiosity with A New Flavor Combination

A classic candy commercial featured two guys walking toward one another on a sidewalk. One was eating a partially unwrapped chocolate bar; the other was carrying an open jar of peanut butter and shoveling it into his mouth with a spoon. Not paying much attention to where they were going, they bumped into one another, causing the chocolate bar to land inside the jar of peanut butter.

When the chocolate eater then pulled out his candy bar, part of it broke off in the jar. At the same time, the part of the bar he was able to remove was slathered with peanut butter. At first, they were both perturbed that there foods had intermingled. But when they then tasted the chocolate and peanut butter combination, they were delighted. Their happy accident had combined two different foods to create a whole new flavor sensation.

Depending on the subject of your speech, you may be able to achieve a similar result by creating a type of speech title that I call the Curious Combo. This requires you to combine two words or concepts that are so different that most people will first experience a bit of a mental jolt in trying to make sense of it. Very much like the jolt that those guys in the commercial experienced when they bumped into one another and saw what they had done.

Not to worry. That is the desired effect of the Curious Combo—to stop people in their tracks and spark their curiosity. They will then be primed to read your subtitle, which will begin to satisfy their curiosity and spell out the value they will gain from your presentation.

The Curious Combo, though, is much more than two seemingly incongruous words or concepts slammed together to get people's attention. The two concepts you choose for this recipe must actually work together to describe or illustrate the core concept for your speech—and possibly your unique take on your subject.

Thus, the initial jolt people get when trying to make sense of your title can be an important first step toward shifting their thinking and moving them into your model of the world. At the same time, they are likely to get the sense that you are an innovative thinker and offer a creative approach to your subject—and they would be right! That, in itself, might prompt them to attend your speech, workshop, or teleclass.

A perfect example of a Curious Combo is the title of the book "Emotional Intelligence" by Daniel Goleman. In this title, Goleman combines two concepts that were traditionally considered to be distinct from one another. You normally think of "emotional" as relating to the realm of feelings and "intelligence" as the ability to think logically and make smart decisions. So when he first introduced the concept of emotional intelligence, I'm sure that a lot of people were initially perplexed. How in the world could intelligence be emotional?

That, though, was exactly the question that Goleman wanted to provoke. His book, after all, focused on redefining and expanding our concept of intelligence. But you didn't have to read the whole book to get that.

Through his simple, two-word Curious Combo title of Emotional Intelligence, he quickly and powerfully made that point and introduced the possibility of thinking about intelligence in a whole new way.

Immediately after his title, Goleman further aroused people's curiosity with the subtitle "Why it can matter more than IQ." Then, to reinforce the paradigm-shifting nature of his work, he added the cover copy "The Groundbreaking Book that Redefines What It Means to be Smart."

Other experts have used a similar Curious Combo approach to get people's attention and expand their understanding of health and healing. Denie and Shelley Hiestand, for instance, wrote a book entitled "Electrical Nutrition," which showed how food affects the electrical system of the human body. For those who hadn't thought of the body as being electrical, this was an eye-opener.

In a similar way, Richard Gerber sought to broaden people's understanding of healing with his book Vibrational Medicine, which explored a range of healing modalities that focused on harmonizing the energetic vibration of the body. If you hadn't thought of medicine as being vibrational, this Curious Combo title certainly got you to consider that possibility. You then, most likely, would be drawn to read Gerber's subtitle "New Choices for Healing Ourselves." This served to further emphasize the notion that he was offering ideas that went beyond the boundaries of conventional medical wisdom.

A Curious Combo title, however, doesn't necessarily have to be used to expand people's thinking about your subject. Sometimes this type of title can be designed to simply get people to see your subject in a novel and memorable way. This, in fact, was the intention of Karen Post, Jeffrey Gitomer, and Michael Tchong with their book entitled "Brain Tatoos: Creating Unique Brands that Stick in Your Customers' Minds."

Here the authors combined two words that you probably had never seen side by side: "brain" and "tattoo." In doing so, they created a striking visual image to help convey the abstract concept of branding. What's more, their title provided a perfect example of that branding concept.

Seth Godin used a similar approach with his book "Purple Cow." Contrary to how it might first appear, this isn't a book about colorful livestock. Godin had simply used this Curious Combo title to provide an example of something that was unusual and remarkable. The reason for this becomes obvious when you read his subtitle: "Transform Your Business by Being Remarkable."

Now that you've had this introduction to the Curious Combo title, it's time to get cooking and come up with one or two of your own. To guide your efforts, here are summaries of the recipes for the two main varieties of the Curious Combo title.

Curious Combo Recipe #1
(To expand people's understanding of your subject.)

1) Find a single word or concept that identifies your subject (e.g. intelligence).

2) Find an adjective you can use with the above topic word to expand people's understanding of your subject (e.g. emotional).

3) Place the adjective in front of the topic word and notice the effect of bringing these two words or concepts together.

4) If you sense that the above combination captures the essence of your program and would spark people's curiosity, create a benefit-focused subtitle that clarifies the title and what your program is about.

5) If your combination title fails to hit the mark, repeat steps 2 and 3 until you have a title that works.

Some examples:

- Emotional Intelligence
- Electrical Nutrition
- Vibrational Medicine

Curious Combo Recipe #2
(To simply get people to see your subject in a novel and memorable way.)

1) Create a clear, specific, benefit-focused speech title that highlights two key elements of your subject. (For example: "Creating Unique Brands that Stick in Your Customers' Minds" Here the key elements are "brands or images that stick," and "minds.")

2) Identify something from another context that is representative or akin to one of the key elements in your title. (For example, for "Unique Brands or Images that Stick," you might come up with postage stamps, name tags, cattle brands, or tattoos.) To find a real winner here, it is a good idea to generate at least a few different possibilities.

3) Turning to the second key element of your working title, come up with at least a few different words or phrases that are representative of it.

4) Pair up the ideas you generated from the two different elements of your working title to see how effectively the combination sparks curiosity and conveys the essence of your speech. (The authors of Brain Tatoos, for instance, might have considered such combinations as brain stamps, brain labels, and brain cattle brands, before finally settling on "Brain Tatoos.")

5) Select the most curious combination that you feel will work best for you.

Some examples:

- Skyrocketing Submarines: Turn Your Deepest Desires into High-Flying Realities
- Silent Screaming: How to Command Attention with Saying a Word
- Leaping Elephants: How to Get Your Biggest Ideas Off the Ground

Ready to play with this? Start simmering your ideas and get curious about what new and provocative flavor combinations you can create with the Curious Combo.

Chapter Sixteen

Stir Things Up with A Shocking Statement

Toss this book into the trash! If I had used this bold statement as the title for this chapter, chances are that it would have piqued your interest even more than the one above. Why? Because it is so bold and unexpected, perhaps even shocking.

Why would I urge you to throw away a book that I had devoted so much time and effort to write? That's the question that my "Toss this book" title would have evoked. To find the answer, you would have to read on.

Natural health expert Dr. Joseph Mercola often uses shocking or provocative titles for the health-related articles he posts on his web site (www.mercola.com). One of his more eye-opening titles, for example, was "Cell Phones are the Cigarettes of the 21st Century."

In this wake-up call of a title, Mercola clearly hints that cell phones pose some real health risks. His apt metaphor also gets you thinking about how else cigarettes and cell phones may be alike. The biggest similarity that might come to mind is that both were widely used before their dangers were generally recognized. But even if you don't immediately get this, the title makes you curious enough to read on.

Naturally, if your speech title leaves people both shocked and perplexed, you will want to add a subtitle that provides a clear, compelling reason for people to attend your presentation. Simply shocking them or making them curious isn't enough. Once you have their attention with your shocker, you will need to show the reason behind the shock, a reason that makes them care about your message.

Here, for example, are a couple of book titles that make use of a shocking title followed by an explanatory subtitle:

People are Idiots and I Can Prove It:
The 10 Ways You are Sabotaging Yourself and How You Can Overcome Them (by Larry Winget)

All Marketers are Liars:
The Power of Telling Authentic Stories in a Low-Trust World (by Seth Godin)

By creating a speech title with shock value, you too can arouse the attention and interest of your target audience. Here is my best recipe for doing just that.

Recipe for the Shocking Speech Title

1) Create an audience-focused subtitle that clearly spells out what your presentation is about.

2) Develop at least a few different bold, outrageous, or surprising statements that are related to the content of your subtitle. What works especially well are hot-headed accusations, angry commands, and curious analogies.

3) Evaluate each of your statements against the following criteria:

    a) Is it bold and provocative?

    b) Does it introduce an element of mystery?

    c) Would it compel the members of your target audience to want to move on to your subtitle?

    d) Is it relevant to your speech topic, without its relevance being totally obvious?

4) Select the title that best satisfies the above criteria.

5) If you're not satisfied with any of your title possibilities, generate more until you find one that works.

And now for something completely different...

—John Cleese

Chapter Seventeen

A Recipe for Rebels: Dole out a Different View

If you approach your speech topic or subject matter in a way that contradicts conventional wisdom, your speech title may be the ideal place to first showcase your contrarian approach. Because your approach is so different, it will immediately stand out. This, in turn, can make people wonder how you could possibly see things so differently or what insights you have that have eluded them.

Let's say, for instance, that you are a time management expert who teaches an unconventional way of managing time. You might use a speech title such as "Toss Your To-Do List and Double Your Productivity."

Since many people have come to believe that to-do lists are the heart of time management, this title would certainly get their attention. At the same time, it would make them wonder "What does this expert know that I don't?"

Here are a few more examples of contrarian titles:

- Contradict Your Boss and Get Promoted
- Snack All Day and Lose Excess Weight
- Lead with Your Weakness
- Spend Your Way to Financial Security

If you are a contrarian or simply have a novel approach to your subject, the recipe for a contrarian speech title should be a very easy one for you to follow. But here it is in two simple steps:

Recipe for a Contrarian Title

1) Create, as your title, a command statement that captures the essence of your contrarian approach.

2) Create a subtitle that conveys the main benefit of following your approach.

Chapter Eighteen

Be Fresh and Unique With Your Signature Dish

There may be many others who speak on your topic. Yet, it's probably safe to say that none of them approach the topic exactly the way that you do. You bring to your topic a distinct perspective, based on your unique experience.

When you share personal experiences during your presentations, you know that you are offering content that only you can deliver and rightfully claim as your own. What might be possible, though, if you could bring that same element of uniqueness into your presentation title? How effectively might that distinguish you from all of the other speakers on your topic?

If you'd like to find out, here's an approach you may want to explore. It simply involves looking at different slices of your experience and seeing if there might be one that has not only helped to shape your unique perspective but could also serve as a framework for helping your audience members see your subject in a new way. More than a starting point for creating a distinctive speech title, this is a way of developing a whole presentation that is unique.

Bill Stainton has used this approach by drawing on his background in television to create a fresh and insightful presentation he delivers to groups of professional speakers. An Emmy Award-winning producer, writer, and performer,

Stainton shows speakers how to think about their presentations from each of these three perspectives. While many other public speaking experts deliver programs on how to polish your presentation, Stainton helps his audience members see their speeches as Hollywood productions. Certainly a fresh approach—and one that helps his audiences of speakers gain deeper insights they can use to master their craft.

And what does Stainton call his program? Simply this: "Enhance Your Presentation: What I Learned from Winning 29 Emmys That Speakers Need to Know." No fancy speech title design tactics here. Just a straight-forward title that states his value proposition, establishes his credibility, and showcases his uniqueness.

Right now, you may be thinking "Sure, this approach is fine if you are an Emmy award winner, an Olympic gold medalist, or an explorer who had just returned from a successful expedition to the North Pole. But I've never achieved anything all that remarkable. How could this approach possibly work for me?"

The good news is that you don't have to earn a major award or achieve something extraordinary to successfully use this approach. That's not the secret sauce here. The key ingredient is your unique perspective based on your life experience and the insights you've gained from the challenges you've overcome along the way.

Mary Jo Rulnick realized this as she mined the gold from her personal experience to establish herself as a speaker and author. Her wealth of experience consisted of a background as a wedding coordinator and event planner and many years as a stay-at-home mom. Hardly a combination that would put her on any Who's Who list (although I'm sure her children would disagree).

Yet by combining what she knew about event planning, entertaining, and child-rearing, Rulnick was able to package her expertise in a way that appealed to mothers who needed better planning skills to simplify their frantic lives. She shared her insights in two books: "The Frantic Woman's Guide to Life" and "The Frantic Woman's Guide to Feeding Family and Friends."

Rulnick was also able to convey her unique positioning platform in the titles of her various workshops which included:

- Feeling Frantic? Simple Steps to Simplify Your Life
- The 15-minute Mom
- The Frantic Cook's Dinner Plan: Zap the Dinnertime Blues
- A Frantic-free Football Bash: An Easy Way to Entertain
- Frantic-free Entertaining

As you can see, Rulnick had no trouble coming up with workshop ideas and titles once she identified the unique perspective that emerged from her experience.

How about you? What have you learned from your personal and/or professional experience that would be of value to your target audience? In particular, what slice of your experience would bring fresh insights to your audiences and expand their thinking about what is possible?

Maybe it is your work experience from a totally different field than that of your target audience. Perhaps it is a long-time hobby, sport, or volunteer activity that has been an important part of your life. Or maybe you have faced a major life challenge and, in the process, have learned lessons that would be valuable to share.

Whatever life has poured into your stock pot of knowledge and experience, this is what you can use to create presentations that have their own special flavor. This is the stock that distinguishes you from other presenters who speak on your topic. This is what makes your perspective unique.

You may need to sift through your range or experiences to find one that serves you best and embodies your unique perspective on your topic. You may need to let different possibilities simmer in your mind for awhile. Or maybe the right one will just naturally bubble up. However you go about it, your goal is to distill your uniqueness through the filter of your experience.

Once you have clearly defined your unique perspective and integrated it with your message, you will have something special to offer your audiences. From that point of clarity, you will also find it easier to create a speech title that both expresses your perspective and enables you to stand out as a speaker.

Part Five

Spices and Seasonings

You will never make your mark as a writer unless you develop a respect for words and a curiosity about their shades of meaning that is almost obsessive. The English language is rich in strong and supple words. Take the time to root around and find the ones you want.

—*William Zinsser*, On Writing Well

Chapter Nineteen

Add Vim and Vigor
With Vital Verbs

I developed a showcase speech that I originally called "Speak and Get Clients." This title worked fairly well for me. It was simple and understandable. It conveyed a clear benefit to my target audience. If you were a professional in need of more clients, it certainly got your attention.

But when I later went to secure "speak and get clients" as an Internet domain name, I was disappointed to discover that it had already been taken. (Obviously, someone else thought that this was an effective title as well.) This then inspired me to consider how I might change my title slightly to one that was still available as a domain name.

After giving this some thought, I came up with a simple idea. Why not just replace the verb "get" with another word that had a similar meaning? Considering different possibilities, I finally settled upon the verb "win." Thus, my new title became "Speak and Win Clients."

I liked it. And I liked it even better when I discovered that it was still available as a domain name, which I quickly secured.

What then struck me was that this new title was so much more expressive than my original one—and all because I had changed a single word. The word "get" was clear and understandable. But my replacement verb "win" added another dimension of feeling and meaning. To "get clients" sounds very cut and dried. But to "win clients" conveys a real sense of victory.

This sense, in fact, was perfectly aligned with the whole spirit and intention behind my showcase speech. My presentation was designed to show professionals how they could win the confidence of potential clients by developing and delivering a value-packed talk to their target audiences. It was all about winning through delivering value. So "win" really was an ideal verb.

When evaluating an action verb in your speech title, consider whether it is as vital and expressive as you want it to be. It doesn't have to be explosive or electrifying. Sometimes a very simple, direct verb (even "get") may work fine and convey just the right about of energy.

Still, it can be well worth it to explore different possible verbs you might use to drive the action in your title or subtitle. Mark Twain reportedly once said that the difference between using the right word and the almost right word can be the difference between lightning and a lightening bug. Since you want your speech title is to grab people's attention, go for the lightning.

A verb such as "increase," for example, expresses the idea of growing in quantity or quality. It doesn't, however, convey the amount or nature of that growth. If you use a title such as "Increase Your Sales," you are simply expressing an outcome that someone could achieve by making one more sale than usual. Hardly an impressive result, unless, of course, you happen to be in the business of selling cruise ships or jumbo jet planes.

If you want to communicate an increase that is dramatic, you might use such verbs as "boost," "rocket," or "double." If, on the other hand, you will be showing your audience members how to increase their sales more slowly and steadily, you might use such verbs as "build" or "grow."

Start by determining the precise meaning and/or feeling you want your verb to express. Then look for a verb that will do that for you. Or simply start generating synonyms for your initial verb and see how they strike you. In that way, you may uncover perfect and precise shades of meaning that you hadn't even considered at first. That, in fact, is exactly how I went from "get" to "win" in creating my "Speak and Win Clients" speech title.

Play with the possibilities and see where they take you. To stimulate your thinking, here are some common verbs used in speech titles, along with different synonyms that express various shades of meaning.

__Common Verb__	__Alternatives__
Attract	draw, magnetize
Avoid	avert, escape, evade, dodge, elude
Beat	overcome, conquer, vanquish, lick
Begin	start, initiate, launch, embark
Benefit	profit, serve, support, empower, enrich, better
Block	thwart, foil, sabotage, impede, stop, barricade, prevent
Change	alter, modify, shift, convert, revamp, transform, re-design, remodel
Choke	strangle, suffocate, throttle

Common Verb	**Alternatives**
Choose	select, pick, adopt, embrace
Consume	devour, eat, swallow
Control	master, rule, dominate, calm
Decrease	lower, drop, chop, lessen, subtract, reduce, shrink, shorten, fall, plummet
Destroy	demolish, ruin, devastate, erase, burn, smash, kill
Do	function, perform, finish, complete
Drain	empty, stop, exhaust, deplete
Engage	enlist, involve, secure, include
Fix	repair, restore, resolve, re-invent, mend, settle
Free	release, unleash, liberate
Gather	amass, accumulate, collect, harvest
Get	gain, grab, nab, win, glean, take, earn, secure, attain, achieve, claim, command, capture
Give	offer, share, relinquish, surrender, donate, present, deliver, grant, award, refund
Handle	tackle, address, resolve, manage

Common Verb	Alternatives
Impress	amaze, astound
Improve	upgrade, update, transform, expand, enrich, rejuvenate, revamp, refine
Increase	raise, boost, double, multiply, soar, skyrocket, climb, grow, build, add
Interest	captivate, fascinate, enthrall, intrigue, engross, engage
Learn	discover, uncover, reveal, master
Like	enjoy, cherish, relish, love, prefer
Lose	forfeit, squander, leak, surrender
Make	create, form, formulate, fashion, produce, invent, devise, prepare, build, craft, shape, design, develop
Motivate	encourage, excite, inspire, mobilize
Move	jump, surge, speed, jet, go, fly, soar
Persuade	sway, convince, induce, sell
Please	gratify, satisfy, thrill, delight
Present	give, deliver, offer, share
Prevent	prohibit, stop, avert
Promote	market, spread, encourage

Common Verb	Alternatives
Protect	guard, safeguard, defend, shelter, shield, preserve, save
Reject	refuse, decline, exclude, discard
Repel	repulse, disgust
Risk	gamble, chance, jeopardize
Run	manage, operate, lead, orchestrate
Show	share, display, highlight, showcase
Stimulate	spark, spur, ignite, jumpstart, stir, awaken, power up, pump up, fire up
Stop	halt, cease, freeze, suspend, curb, block, end, terminate, short-circuit
Struggle	strive, strain, battle, fight, flounder
Suffer	agonize, endure, tolerate
Succeed	thrive, prosper, flourish, grow, triumph, win, excel, shine

Chapter Twenty

Whet Their Appetite: Stimulate the Senses

We experience the world through our five senses of sight, hearing, touch, taste, and smell. We also think about our experiences to process and analyze what is going on. But it is our senses that enliven our thoughts and at times help spur us to action.

Ideally, you want your speech title to be much more than a string of lifeless words on a page. You want it to light up people's imagination like a fireworks display, to sing to their spirit, or to make them tingle with curiosity and excitement. You may even want your title to give people a whiff of the sweet smell of success or to convey a possibility that is so mouth-watering that they can almost taste it.

All of this is possible when you create a speech title that engages the senses. This, in turn, can motivate meeting planners to book you to speak and your ideal target audience members to flock to your program.

This doesn't necessarily mean that you need to fashion your speech title into a festival for the senses. I did this two paragraphs ago simply to highlight the range of possibilities for bringing sensory experience into your writing. If you go overboard like this in your speech title, you just might send people into sensory overload. This could leave them feeling like they had just attended a wild party the night before and couldn't remember what happened when they woke up the next morning.

To add spark to your speech title, you may, in fact, need to involve only one or two of the senses. The trick is in determining what will work best for your purposes and what will resonate most deeply with your target audience.

Of our five senses, sight, hearing, and touch (or feeling) are the most predominant and can be most easily harnessed in crafting a speech title. If you are a chef who speaks about cooking, of course, you'd have no trouble also bringing the senses of taste and smell into your title.

If you're a sales coach, on the other hand, you may be stretching it if you create a speech title such as "How to Smell When a Prospect is Ready to Buy," unless, of course, you are also an expert on human pheromones. More within the bounds of reason, however, might be a title such as "How to Get Your First Big Taste of Sales Success."

While the senses of smell and taste can, in the right contexts, have great appeal, you will generally find it easier to draw more appropriate and effective sensory-based language from the realms of sight, hearing, and touch (or feeling). Still, remain open to all possibilities for engaging the senses.

Here is a sampling of words and phrases you might use in your speech title to appeal to different senses.

Visual

Verbs: see, look, view, watch, show, peak, focus, picture, illuminate, envision, highlight, brighten, darken, color

Adjectives: colorful (and actual colors), bright, light, clear, huge, giant, tiny, straight, crooked, jagged

Phrases: shine the spotlight, see results, focus on priorities, picture the possibilities, bright as a summer's day, spot the signal, watch your sales soar, blinding flash of brilliance

Auditory

Verbs: hear, listen, sound, sizzle, sing, tell, describe, announce, attune, voice, cheer, speak, whisper, shout, ring

Adjectives: musical, rhythmic, screeching, thunderous, whispering, churning, cheering, sizzling

Phrases: ring a bell, cheer on your team, meet with thunderous applause, applaud your success

Kinesthetic (internal and external feeling)

Verbs: feel, touch, grasp, hold, handle, rub, grab, embrace, clutch, tap, motivate, excite, inspire

Adjectives: cool, cold, frozen, warm, hot, scorching, heavy, light, smooth, rough, dull, sharp, scary, calming, heart-warming, exciting, confident, enthusiastic, pressing

Phrases: grab your attention, embrace change, inspire your team, conquer your fear, unleash your confidence

Movement (a stimulant of feeling)

Verbs: soar, struggle, shoot, rush, glide, slide, slip, race, rock, roll, run, propel, push, pull, plummet, drop, stretch, twist, tumble, fall, drive, coast, leap, jump, kick, pump

Adjectives: End the verbs above with "ing."

Phrases: propel yourself to success, pump up your productivity, stretch your imagination, kick into action, get over it, snap out of it, push through your resistance, get around your obstacles, move beyond your limitations

Taste

Verbs: taste, savor, salivate, sweeten, eat, drink, swallow, nibble, devour, lick, bite

Adjectives: sweet, sour, bitter, salty, savory, delicious, spicy, mouth-watering, bland

Phrases: savor your success, spice up your meetings, uncover what's eating you, face the bitter truth, sweeten your company's incentive program

Smell

Verbs: smell, sniff, inhale, breathe, reek

Adjectives: fragrant, sweet, aromatic, scented, reeking

Phrases: sniff out trouble, catch the scent, reeking of deception, sweet smell of success

Chapter Twenty-One

Ear Candy:
Make It Sound Sweet

Speech writers, lyricists, and poets have something in common. They all focus on harnessing the sound and rhythm of language to bring their message to life. As they write, they listen to their words to hear how they play out. As they review and revise their work, they listen even more closely to get a sense of whether or not their words ring true and can be easily absorbed by their readers or listeners.

To write an effective speech title, you must do the same. Naturally, you want to begin by clarifying what you want to say. Once you have figured that out, however, it is time to fine-tune how you want to say it.

This is your opportunity to play with the sound and the rhythm of language to write a speech title that resonates with your target audience. So let's look at some different ways that you might do that.

Attract Attention with Alliteration

When you combine two or more words that begin with the same sound, you are alliterating. Why might you want to do this in a speech title? Besides being generally pleasing to the ear, alliteration tends to heighten your attention and allow your words to be more easily comprehended.

Compare the word pair "troublesome boy," for example, with the pair "bad boy." Both convey a similar idea. Yet, the phrase "bad boy" is much easier to grasp.

Much of this greater ease of comprehension is related to the fact that the two words in this phrase begin with same sound, which makes them easier to absorb. Another factor, however, is that both "bad" and "boy" are short and simple words. The more clear and simple you make the words in your alliterative phrases, the more you will accentuate the power of alliteration.

Some examples of possible alliterative speech titles:

- How to Make Money in the Market
- Build Relationships that Bring You Business
- Ten Tactics for Speaking Success

Rhyme Time Can be Sublime

Best-selling children's book author Dr. Seuss made much more than a dime from the power of rhyme. He built his whole reputation on it. In such children's classics as "The Cat in the Hat" and "Yertle the Turtle," he used rhyme to engage his young readers and to help them have fun along the way.

Modeling the good doctor, you may be able to harness the power of rhyme to create speech titles that connect with your target audience and, at the same time, capture a sense of playfulness. You don't need to be a poet to do this.

Just be willing to play a bit and explore some rhyming possibilities among the words related to your speech topic.

Some examples of possible speech titles that make use of rhyme:

- How to Survive and Thrive in the Business Jungle
- How Food Affects Your Mood
- Make Money from Being Funny

Of course, you want to use your discretion in how you make use of rhyme or even in deciding if it will work for you. After all, you don't want to make rhymes that sound forced or overly cutesy or distract people from what you are trying to say. But if you can find two or more rhyming words that convey key elements of your topic, you may be able to create a speech title that sings.

Make a Play on Words

Using creative word play in your speech title can engage people with a sense of light-heartedness. Just make sure that you clearly communicate the central theme of your speech and don't sacrifice clarity for the sake of being cute or clever.

Wellness expert Jan Krouskop effectively used creative word play in her speech title "Beat Burnout Before...You Are Toast." This title may have just come to her in a flash of inspiration. But if she did use a more methodical approach to developing this title, it probably involved asking and answering 3 simple questions:

1. What are some core words or phrases related to my topic of stress? ("Burnout" would be one of these.)

2. What words or phrases have some relevance or connection to the words on my first list? (Looking for words or phrases related to "burnout," she considered what all could be "burned out," with "toast" coming to mind.)

3. How can I make a creative connection between a core word on my first list and a related word or phrase on my second list? (Here she came up with the common phrase "You are toast," which is actually the vernacular for being stressed out.)

Another way to bring word play into your title is to take a common phrase and replace a key word in the phrase with another word that not only sounds like the word you are replacing but gives the phrase a new meaning that captures the essence of your speech topic. Here, for example, are two speech titles that professional speakers have crafted using this approach.

Everything's Coming Up Neurosis
Michael Broome, Motivational Humorist

The Brand Canyon – the Relationship between Experience Management & Brand Management
Lou Carbone, The Business Experience Movement

In the first example above, humorist Michael Broome took the common phrase "Everything's coming up roses" and replaced the word "roses" with the similar-sounding word "neurosis." This not only gave his speech title a familiar sound but added a twist of humor that also conveyed the humorous nature of his presentation.

In the second example, marketing speaker Lou Carbone took the well-known phrase "Grand Canyon" and replaced the word "grand" with the similar-sounding word "brand." He then created a subtitle that made the concept of a "brand canyon" relevant to his topic of branding.

To experiment with this approach to word play, first identify one or two key words related to your speech topic. Then come up with a list of other words that sound similar to your key words. As you look at each of these similarly sounding words, try to think of a common phrase that contains it. One of these phrases could very well serve as your speech title. Then, all you need is a subtitle that clarifies the meaning of your altered phrase and relates your topic to the needs or interests of your target audience.

It may take several attempts to come up with a phrase that works as an effective title and you may not accomplish this in a single sitting. But if you embrace the intention to find a common phrase that could be easily altered to form an appropriate title for your presentation, your unconscious mind will be on the lookout for just the right phrase. Then, when you happen to hear someone use that phrase or you come across it in something you are reading, it will leap out at you. So be ready for that to happen.

If you love to play with words, you can have a lot of fun with language. But if this isn't your game, that's fine too. This book contains plenty of other speech title ideas you can put to work or play.

Find Your Fascinating Rhythm

A popular song may have clever, meaningful lyrics and a catchy combination of notes. But there is more behind its popularity than that. It also has an underlying rhythm that drives the music and may even have you tapping your foot in time to the beat.

An effective speech title also has a certain compelling rhythm to it. Because it works with words, often quite subtly, people may not even be aware of it. All they know is that the title rings true. If, however, a speech title lacks rhythm, the words and the message become more difficult to swallow and digest.

Each January, the U.S. President delivers his State of the Union Address to update the American people about how the country is doing. The speech title "State of the Union" has a natural rhythm to it and easily rolls off the tongue.

But what if instead this speech was called the "How the United States is Doing Right Now" address? While the words in this title are certainly clear and understandable, they don't ride a natural wave of rhythm as is the case in the title "State of the Union." And can you imagine how much this alternative title would have reporters and commentators tripping over their tongues?

If the President is ever looking to change or revise his speech title, I might suggest the title "United States Update," which has a rhyming quality, a musical rhythm, and is a little more clear, specific, and understandable than "State of the Union." Of course, since the rhythmic quality and purpose of the title "State of the Union" has already been anchored into the American consciousness, he is probably just as well to stick with that.

Ideally, you want to create a speech title that not only communicates a clear message but has a rhythm that helps to drive home that message. To do that, you want to give your title a form that helps it perform.

One powerful way to infuse a sense of rhythm into your title is to make use of parallel construction. Whenever your title contains two main phrases or clauses, you simply make sure that the two phrases (or clauses) have an identical form. If, for example, one phrase consists of a verb followed by a noun, then the other should as well. It is the repetition of form that helps to drive the rhythm.

See and hear how this works in the following sample titles that employ parallel construction.

- Write Your Book to Boost Your Credibility
- Speak with Authority, Lead with Confidence
- Six Steps to Help You Look Good and Feel Great
- Command the Creativity of a Child and the Artistry of a Master
- Cook Like a Chef, Dine Like a King

Do you get a sense of the rhythm in each of these titles? As you're fine-tuning your next speech title, play with parallel construction and harness the power of rhythm.

If those who have studied the art of writing are in accord on any one point, it is on this: the surest way to arouse and hold the attention of the reader is by being specific, definite, and concrete.

—*William Strunk, Jr.*, The Elements of Style

Chapter Twenty-Two

Spice it Up
with Specificity

If your speech title seems too bland, you may be able to give it a spicy kick by adding a dash of specificity. This simply involves transforming a vague, general concept into one that is more clear and specific.

What's really eating your audience?

One way to make your title more specific is to express a specific negative result of a key issue you address in your speech. Don't simply convey a vague reason for the pain or frustration of your target audience members. Be specific as possible about what is really eating them.

Starting with the title "How to Handle Customer Dissatisfaction," for example, ask yourself this question: What is a specific negative result of having dissatisfied customers? One likely result is that they will not return to buy from you again. In addition, they won't recommend your business to people they know. Even worse, they may bad-mouth your business to their friends and family, effectively damaging your reputation.

Highlighting the first of these negative results and bringing in a number for specificity, you might re-write the above title as: "The Five Biggest Reasons That Many First-time Customers Never Return to Buy from You Again." Focusing on a different negative result, you might use the title "The Real Reasons Your Customers Aren't Referring Their Friends to Your Business." Or another possibility: "How to Address the Real Reasons that Some of Your Customers Bad-mouth Your Business."

Each of these titles expresses a specific negative result of having dissatisfied customers. They don't just mention that the speaker will address the "problem" of customer dissatisfaction. They clearly spell out what the real problem is, leaving no doubt as to how it is a problem.

Can you see how much more appealing any of these titles are than the more vague and general title "How to Handle Customer Dissatisfaction?"

Sure, it is reasonable to assume that most anyone in business could figure out how and why customer dissatisfaction is a problem. But if you are a speaker seeking to get booked to speak and attract an audience, do you really want to force people to figure out for themselves why your topic is important to them?

Of course, people could do this. As a rule, though, they don't. They don't view a speech title as a puzzle to be figured out. They want to look at the title and get an immediate sense that there is something in that speech for them, as well as a clear idea of what that something is. If your title doesn't evoke that kind of instant response in the people you want to reach, you will most likely lose them.

Magnify the Pain and Gain

Pain and gain are the major factors that motivate people to take action. The more you can intensify these factors in your title, the more compelling or enticing your appeal will be. One of the most powerful ways to do this is to get clear and specific.   Exactly, how much pain could someone experience if they don't resolve the issue that is the focus of your presentation?   Or how much, in very specific terms, could someone benefit from the ideas you have to share?

In each of the following pairs of speech titles, the first conveys an issue or outcome in a general way, while the second incorporates a number or quantifying word to add an element of specificity. Notice the difference.

- Common Habits that Lower Your Life Expectancy
- Common Habits that Can Cut 10 or More Years from Your Life

- Identify Financial Leaks in Your Business
- Identify Financial Leaks in Your Business that May Cost You Hundreds of Dollars Each Year

- Boost Your Energy
- Double Your Energy

- Increase Your Productivity
- Accomplish Twice as Much in Half the Time

- How to Get Free Publicity
- How to Get Thousands in Free Publicity

As you can see, by referring to a number or quantity, you can effectively intensify the severity of the pain or the allure of the gain. At the same time, this doubles or even triples the selling power of your title.

America is a country that doesn't know where it is going
but is determined to set a speed record getting there.

—*Laurence J. Peter*

Chapter Twenty-Three

Feed Their
Need for Speed

In the popular 1986 film Top Gun, Tom Cruise played a U.S. Navy fighter pilot who uttered a line that was ranked by the American Film Institute as one of the top all-time quotations in American cinema. The line: "I feel the need—the need for speed!"

What made this line so catchy? It was more than the use of rhythm and rhyme. This line struck a chord that resonated with the American consciousness. Life was moving at an accelerating pace—and this short, simple, compelling line conveyed the desire or even the need for speed that so many people felt.

We live in an age where if you ask someone when they would like something done, the typical answer is "yesterday." We have fast food, overnight mail delivery, on-demand movies, and instant messaging. We want results and we want them fast.

With this in mind, you can make your speech title more compelling by appealing to your target audience's need for speed. You can do this by emphasizing how quickly people can achieve what they want by applying what they learn from your presentation.

Some examples of speed-infused titles:

- Cut Your Income Tax Preparation Time in Half
- How to Lose 10 Pounds in 30 Days
- Double Your Energy in Less Than a Week
- How to Get More Done in Less Time
- Triple Your Reading Speed
- Accelerate the Return on Your Investments
- How to Speed Up Your Sales Cycle

Two highly successful books that have appealed to people's need for speed include: The One-Minute Manager by Ken Blanchard and Spencer Johnson and The Four-Hour Work Week by Timothy Ferris. In fact, the "speed" angle worked so well for Blanchard and Ferris that they each followed up with books that also put the spotlight on speed. Blanchard teamed up with other authors to write such books as The One-Minute Negotiator and The On-Time, On-Target Manager. Ferris's follow-up books included: The 4-Hour Body and the 4-Hour Chef.

Since a focus on speed and fast results worked so well for these best-selling authors, just maybe this is an element that you will want to bring into your speech title as well. So what are you waiting for?

Part Six

Setting the Table for Meeting Planners

My greatest strength as a consultant is to
be ignorant and ask a few questions.

—*Peter Drucker*

Chapter Twenty-Four

Uncover What They Crave

Whether you want to speak at a corporate or association event, you and your speech title must first spark the interest of a meeting planner. If you are booked to speak at an association event, you also want your title to help motivate the association's members to attend your program. Still, your first sale is to the meeting planner.

How do you create a speech title that helps you make that sale? You could simply follow any number of the speech title recipes in this book and have a good shot at it. Quite often, though, making this sale requires more than whipping up a speech title using a randomly selected recipe and hoping for the best. It requires you to embrace the mindset of the meeting planner and use that perspective to guide you in selecting just the right recipe, combination of recipes, or ingredients to make your title a winner.

If a meeting planner tells you upfront exactly what kind of presentation he or she is looking for and your existing speech or workshop title plugs right into that description, there may be little or nothing you need to do to tweak your title. If, however, you don't fully understand the nature and needs of the organization and the event, you would be wise to do a little research to help you tailor your title.

How to Research an Association

When first contacting a meeting planner about the possibility of speaking at an upcoming association event, you can do some basic research by asking a few targeted questions to learn more about the organization and its needs. To start, you might ask such questions as:

- If there is a theme for your meeting, what is it?
- Currently, what are the association members' most pressing problems in relation to my topic?
- What is the make-up of the audience? (age, gender, occupation, experience level)
- What other presentations on my topic has the organization sponsored?
- How do you want your group members to be different after hearing my presentation?

You can often gather further valuable intelligence by visiting the organization's web site. There you can learn about the group's mission and values. You may also find a listing of the featured presentations at the organization's past or upcoming meeting programs.

Review the titles of these presentations. Notice how these titles are structured and focused. See what types of issues these titles address and what types of appeals they make. While many of these titles may be far from ideal, they were good enough to interest the group in booking the program. With that in mind, look for clues as to how you might tailor your speech title to capture the interest of both the meeting planner and the group.

Chapter Twenty-Five

Key Ingredients to Give Your Title an Edge

While there is no standard recipe for creating a speech title that will appeal to every meeting planner, there are certain ingredients that have been proven to be most effective. Using what you know about an organization and its programming needs, you can blend some or all of these ingredients into a speech title that makes the meeting planner salivate (or at least be interested enough to read the rest of your program description).

What are these key ingredients? They include value, relevance, timeliness, and uniqueness. Let's take a closer look at each of these.

Value: A Core Ingredient

First and foremost, meeting planners look for speech and workshop titles that communicate value. They want to see at least one clear, compelling benefit to their members or meeting attendees.

If your speech is inspirational, they will want your speech title to have an inspirational flavor and provide a clear sense of what you will be inspiring people to do. If your program is more informative or educational, they will expect your title or subtitle to spell out how their group will benefit from what you have to teach. If your speech is primarily entertaining, they will want your title to convey a sense of fun and promise their group a good time.

Whatever value your presentation brings to a group or organization, your title must make it crystal clear.

Relevance: Is your program a good fit?

If you give a dry crust of bread to a hungry man, you have offered him something valuable to help satisfy his hunger. If, however, you give him the type of food that he craves the most, you have presented him with a treat that he will eagerly devour. You have gone beyond a mere offering of value and given him something that is relevant to his deepest desires.

This is also your objective in creating or tweaking a speech title that will appeal to meeting planners. You may be competing for a speaking opportunity against many other speakers, each with his or her own offering of value. Everything else being equal, the speaker whose offering is most relevant to the needs of the organization is the one who will land the speaking engagement.

One powerful way to show relevance in your speech title is to shine your focus on your target audience members and, if possible, one of their particular challenges. If you are a sales trainer who wants to speak to a group of real estate agents, you could offer a presentation called "How to Sell Anything to Anybody." Since your target audience members are involved in sales, your program would certainly be a fit on that count. The trouble is that this title is so generic that they may doubt that your program would be of much value in addressing their particular selling challenges.

So instead, let's say that you titled your presentation "How to Sell More Houses to Couples." With this title, it is clear that your presentation is specifically for real estate agents. What's more, by narrowing your focus to "selling to couples," something of great potential interest to many real estate agents, you have made your title even more relevant to your target audience.

Of course, this assumes that you are willing and able to tailor your material to your audience. If you specialize in speaking to a certain type of audience, though, you've already done that. And if that's the case, why hide it? Showcase your specialization in your program title and you will instantly connect with both the meeting planner and your target audience.

Timeliness: Is now the right time?

Want to give your speech title an extra competitive edge? Find a way to convey the timeliness of your message or presentation. Why is your talk especially relevant to the needs of your target audience right now? Why should a meeting planner book you to speak now rather than next year? What would prompt a meeting planner to schedule your talk immediately rather than throwing your speaking proposal into a "someday" pile?

After the attacks on the United States on September 11, 2001, the whole nation was in a state of shock. Airline travel suddenly declined. The hotel and hospitality industry also took a hit, as more and more people were afraid to travel and leave home. Due to increased security concerns, airlines instituted a more rigorous process for screening passengers, adding to the difficulty of traveling.

During this period of heightened fear and uncertainty, there was an increased need for guidance about how to function in a world that had suddenly changed. Security had become a timely issue. As a result, meeting planners, especially those in the travel and hospitality industries, were on the lookout for speakers and trainers who showed that they were ready to address that issue. Realizing this, many savvy speakers began tweaking their speech titles to make it clear that they were in touch with the current security concerns of their audiences.

Naturally, at any given moment, not every speech topic will be particularly timely. But if you can craft a speech title that shows or implies the timeliness of your topic, you will have yet another way of commanding a meeting planner's attention.

To help prime your thinking, here are some different elements you might bring into play to give your topic a sense of timeliness:

- A major world event (e.g. the Olympics)
- A significant news item
- An approaching season (tax, election, holiday)
- Current economic climate
- New laws affecting an industry
- Upcoming change in tax laws
- Recent changes within an industry
- Hot new trend

Find a way to bring timeliness into your speech title and you will let meeting planners know that now is the time to book you as a speaker.

Uniqueness: What makes you different?

How are you different from others who speak on your topic? What makes your presentation stand out in a positive way? What makes your program or your approach to your topic unique? These are questions that meeting planners are either consciously or unconsciously asking when they are reviewing your speaking proposal.

Meeting planners are often looking for presentations that are a little or a lot different than their standard fare. It is, of course, a given that they want programs that address issues that are highly relevant to their attendees. But at the same time, they are seeking speakers who bring a fresh perspective or approach to those issues.

Earlier in this book, we looked at four different ways that you can give your speech title a stamp of uniqueness and a sense of your fresh perspective. To quickly recap, these included:

1) **Metaphor:** Likening your topic to another subject or realm of experience to help give people a deeper understanding of your topic (as in the title of John Gray's best-selling book "Men are from Mars, Women are from Venus").

2) **The Curious Combo:** Combining two seemingly incongruous words or concepts to convey your subject in a novel and memorable way and possibly expand people's understanding of it (as in the book titles: Emotional Intelligence, Electrical Nutrition, Vibrational Medicine, and Brain Tatoos.)

3) **The Contrarian Approach:** Stating something that is the direct opposite of conventional wisdom (as with a time management expert giving a speech entitled "Toss Your To-Do List!").

4) **The Experienced-based Approach:** Using your experience from a different but similar field to help your target audience members see your topic from a fresh perspective (as with Bill Stainton's program "Enhance Your Presentation: What I Learned from Winning 29 Emmys that Speakers Need to Know").

The common ingredient in all four of these speech title recipes is originality, innovative thinking that promises to expand people' understanding of a topic, leading them to deeper insights and a fresh perspective. Of course, this is not the kind of thinking that you just whip up when it is time to create a title for your presentation. It is what goes into the process of developing the presentation itself.

When your presentation is defined by original thinking, the process of titling it is then simply a matter of distilling the essence of that thinking in a provocative way. What's important is that you understand what makes your approach to your topic different, what gives it an edge. Only when you understand that will you be ready to create a title that captures and expresses your uniqueness.

You are now familiar with the four key ingredients of value, relevance, timeliness, and uniqueness. Use them wisely, apply your creative cooking skills and voila—you will have a title that whets the appetite of the most discerning meeting planner.

Part Seven

Master the Creative
Cooking Process

Illumination comes while coasting, but coasting inescapably implies that *power* has been *previously* applied.

—*Alex Osborn,* Your Creative Power

Chapter Twenty-Six

Stir and Simmer Your Creativity

If you are naturally creative or have highly developed creative powers, you know that much of your success in generating great ideas is related to your confidence in your ability to do so. Even the most clever and innovative people will draw a blank or come up empty if they approach a creative task in a state of doubt or helplessness. But when they stay positive and excited about the task at hand and embrace the belief that they have the ability to create something remarkable, their excitement and belief come together like flint and steel to spark their imagination and light their creative fire.

Whether or not you consider yourself to be a highly creative person, you are—and you have the potential to develop your creative power even further. The fact that you are reading this book indicates that, most likely, you have already exercised tremendous creativity in developing a presentation that you want to share in a bigger way with your target audience. You were excited enough about your topic to develop a presentation about it. Now, you simply need to channel that excitement into the creative task of developing a more compelling title for your talk.

Just as there are both fast and slow approaches to cooking, so it is in the realm of creating a winning speech title. Your mind, in essence, can function as both a microwave oven and a slow-cooking crock pot. Your success as a speech title chef depends on your ability to use both of these modes of cooking up titles. So let's look at how you can become skilled at each of these approaches.

The Microwave Oven Method

After you've done your initial prep work of defining your target audience and clarifying the major benefit and most pressing issue or issues you want to address in your title, you will first want to shift into the microwave mode. This involves channeling your creative power, in a very focused way, to generate some possible titles.

Here is a brief summary of how to turn on your mental microwave oven and put this approach into action:

1) Create a working title for your presentation as described earlier.

2) Select from this book a speech title recipe that you feel may be a good fit for your presentation.

3) Ask yourself with a sense of confident expectation to come up with a title that embodies the essence of your recipe.

4) See what pops up in your mind and write it down.

5) Repeat steps 3 and 4 to generate other possible titles. (To harness your full creative power, shoot for 15-20 different titles.)

There are 3 keys to success in using this approach:

1) You must be clear about what you want to communicate in your title.
2) You must be excited or enthusiastic about what you want to say.
3) You must command a state of total confidence in your ability to generate a winning title.

This is not the time to be analytical. You have already done your analytical work upfront in analyzing your audience and figuring out the core ideas you want to convey. This is the time to call upon your vast unconscious reservoir of creative intelligence to allow the kind of title you are requesting to naturally surface.

You may have heard the saying "Ask and you shall receive." That's exactly what you are doing here. But you are not just asking and hoping for an answer. You are asking in a state of positive, confident expectation that the answer will come. It is your ability to command this state that creates the pathway for an answer to appear.

When a title comes to you, write it down immediately. It doesn't matter if it's not perfect. You're not going for perfection at this point. You're simply seeing how many creative possibilities you can generate and clearing your mind of the ones that are less than perfect.

This, in turn, will give your mind the creative space it needs to uncover title possibilities that are even better than the ones that first surface. Also, once you get a number of different titles down on paper, it will be easier for you to see what works and what doesn't, as well as how you might creatively combine elements from different titles. Even a title that is obviously a dud may open your mind to the possibility of one that is truly inspired.

If you haven't exercised your creative muscles in awhile, this approach may take some effort to produce the results that you want. With practice, however, your creative confidence will build as you become more skilled at harnessing the power of your mind.

To many, this approach may seem like nothing short of magic. If you regularly exercise your creativity and imagination, however, you know that this is simply a way of directing your unconscious mind to do all of the real creative work and then clearing the way for the finished product to pop out.

The Crock Pot Approach

If you try the microwave oven approach to developing speech titles and are disappointed with the results, relax. Sure, it is possible to come up with a brilliant speech title in a single sitting. But quite often you need to give your mind more time in order to fully harness its creative power. Rather than thinking of your mind as a microwave oven that can cook up ideas in a jiffy, it is often more useful to treat your mind as a slow-cooking crock pot.

When you give your mind the time to fully consider different creative alternatives, to allow your ideas to simmer, to make connections that only come after the stewing of a slow-cook process, you open yourself to the possibility of generating ideas that are truly inspired.

Of course, in developing a speech title, you don't have to choose between the microwave method and the crock pot approach. In fact, you will generally get the best results if you include both approaches in your creative process. Unlike the cooking of food, where fast and slow cooking are two separate options, the cooking of ideas actually requires you to use the fast-cook (or microwave) method in order to set the slow-cook crock pot approach into motion. It is, after all, your initial intense burst of conscious creative effort that signals your unconscious mind to start working on your creative task at a much deeper level.

You must then allow your mind the time and space it needs to do this vital creative work, while being clear that you will check in later to see how everything is coming along. When you relax and give your mind the freedom it needs to work its creative magic, you may even find that inspired ideas will just pop into your consciousness unbeckoned, before you've even had a chance to check back in. But even if this doesn't happen, you will likely find that when you do return to your creative task in a conscious way, fresh ideas and insights will start bubbling to the surface and you will see creative possibilities that weren't at all obvious to you at first.

Summary of the Crock Pot Approach

1) Use the Microwave Oven Method to generate some initial speech title possibilities and prime your mind for further creative activity.

2) When you finish your microwave creative session, ask your unconscious mind to come up with an even better title than anything you have so far. In a state of confident, positive expectation, ask yourself "What is the best possible title for my talk?"

3) Embrace the intention that your unconscious mind will slow-cook different creative possibilities outside your awareness to find an answer to your question and deliver it when the cooking process is complete.

4) Shift your attention to something else, perhaps an activity that requires little or no mental effort, allowing your unconscious mind to work, on its own, on the task you have given it.

5) If a new speech title pops into your consciousness, write it down. Then, in the same positive, expectant state that you embraced earlier, ask your mind to come up with something even better and send it on its way to work its creative magic.

6) If no new speech title possibilities come to you as you are going about your life, that's fine. Just be ready to see what naturally bubbles up when you next sit down to work on this creative task.

7) To more fully activate your unconscious creativity, assign your mind its creative task just before you go to sleep at night. In a confident state of positive expectation, give yourself a suggestion such as this: "As I sleep peacefully tonight, my mind will develop the perfect title for my presentation." Then, the next morning, be ready to see what comes to you.

By practicing and mastering this slow-cook crock pot creative process, you will not only find it easier and easier to create compelling speech titles, you will develop the ability to more effectively tackle almost any creative challenge. And who knows where that will take you?

Chapter Twenty-Seven

How to Taste-Test and Tweak Your Titles

Once you have generated a number of possible titles using the microwave oven method and/or crock pot approach, you still need to answer a couple of important questions. First, how do you evaluate all of these titles and pick one that will work best for you? Second, how do you take the most promising title and transform it into something even more compelling?

It is possible that, without you doing any formal analysis or evaluation, one of your title choices may just naturally stand out as being better than the rest. You have the sense that it captures the essence of your presentation and would resonate with your target audience. Take note of this feeling. If you are clear about the value of your presentation and have a deep understanding of your target audience, this feeling can be a signal that a title will work well for you.

Just to be sure, though, you can then compare this title to each of the other titles you've created to see how it stacks up. If, in each case, it feels like a clear winner, you've been able to quickly narrow your choices to the one that naturally seems best. If, on the other hand, you have some question about which of two titles is better, you will want to stop and do some analysis.

Often when speakers reach this point, they snap into an endless loop of indecision. They go back and forth between two titles that they like equally well, perhaps for slightly different reasons. Then, after mentally wearing themselves out, they just pick the one that feels a little better and let go of the other.

Fortunately, there is a less stressful and more scientific way of choosing between two titles. It involves asking and answering some questions, questions that will help you clear your mental fog and dissolve your decision-making dilemma, questions that will enable you to clarify and understand the underlying strengths and weaknesses of the titles you are considering, questions that can spur you to uncover creative possibilities that you might never have found otherwise. Here they are.

The Magic Comparison Questions

1) Which title more clearly and simply conveys the essence of my presentation to my target audience?

2) Which title would be more compelling to my target audience?

3) Which title will more quickly grab the attention of my target audience?

4) Is there any way that elements of two titles might be combined to create one that would be even more appealing to my target audience?

As you can see, all of these questions force you to look at your title choices through the eyes of your target audience.

If you stay stuck inside your own head, it can be difficult to judge how well a title will work. But when you make the effort to look through different perceptual filters of your audience, you will start to command a whole new ability to evaluate and fine-tune the titles that you create.

What do you do, though, if you get mixed answers to the first three magic questions when comparing one title with another? What if one title is more clear and compelling while the other is more attention-grabbing? Or what if there is no clear winner in regard to one or more of the criteria? Wouldn't that still leave you unsure about which one to choose?

It could if you stopped your investigative thinking process right there. On the other hand, if you play the role of a detective and then ask why, in relation to each magic question, one title is better than another, you will start to uncover clues that can continue to fuel your creative process. Rather than just relying on which title feels better, which is a great place to start, you are digging in and pulling out the underlying reasons that one title works better than another. This, in turn, can give you some insight into what you need to do to improve a title that is not quite as effective as it could be.

Had you simply declared one title the winner because it was stronger on most counts, you would have missed this opportunity for improvement. This is why it is so important to generate several possible titles and then bring critical, analytical thinking into your creative process. It is after all, the interplay between your creative mind and your analytical mind that enables you to produce the best possible result.

How to Make a Good Title Better

Let's say that you have created a title that you feel is clearly the best of all the possibilities you have generated. At this point, you could just stop and be done with it. Still, there could be some room for improvement. And since your title is the magnet that can help you attract an audience, doesn't it make sense for you to do whatever you can to make that magnet as powerful as possible?

With this in mind, here is a two-phase process you can use to explore the possibilities of making your good title even better. The first phase simply involves asking a slight variation of 3 of the core magic questions we've already considered. These other improvement-focused questions include:

1) What, if anything, could I change to make this title even more clear to my target audience?

2) What, if anything, could I change, to make this title more compelling to my target audience? (In other words, how could I possibly beef up the benefit or pump up the problem I highlight?)

3) What, if anything, could I change to make this title more powerfully grab the attention of my target audience?

If these questions help you come up with improvements, great. If not, that's fine too. That may just indicate that you had a solid title to begin with.

In either case, you can then move on to the second phase of your fine-tuning process. This involves evaluating your title in relation to the areas addressed in the Spices and Seasonings section of this book. In question form, these areas are as follows:

1) Could you use more vital verbs?
2) How could this title better stimulate the senses?
3) How might you improve the sound of your title in such areas as alliteration, rhyme, word play, and rhythm?
4) How might you make your title more specific?
5) How might you alter your title slightly to appeal to people's need for speed?

Of course, you don't need to make changes based on all of these questions. Perhaps your particular audience has no great "need for speed." Or maybe word play or rhyme isn't a fit for what you are trying to communicate. That's fine. The purpose of these questions is simply to open your mind to a range of possible areas for improvement.

The Value of Outside Feedback

Once you have worked your creative magic to develop a title you like, you may feel ready to serve it up to your target audience. If you have followed the guidelines outlined in this book, you will certainly have a title that is much better than what you started with. You have identified certain key ingredients, blended them together, cooked them in the oven or crock pot of your mind, and added spices to bring out just the right flavor. You may even find the final result to be absolutely delectable.

The only question is—can you trust your own taste buds? Will your target audience find your title to be as appealing as you do? Or somewhere along the way, might you have fallen in love with your creation and let that blind you to one or more of its flaws?

By objectively asking and answering the evaluation questions in this chapter, you can shed light on what may have been blind spots for you. Still, it may not be possible to be totally objective or to view your title in exactly the way that your target audience would. This is why even professional writers rely on editors and proofreaders to review their writing.

To benefit from an outside perspective, you too may want to show your "best choice" titles to others and get their feedback. To secure the most helpful feedback, though, make sure that the people you approach are representative of your target audience or have a deep understanding of that audience. Otherwise, their responses may be no more helpful than the opinion of someone who has never gone fishing as to which fishing pole he likes best. (Oh, I like the dark green one. After all green is my favorite color.)

In eliciting feedback, pre-frame your request by clearly specifying who your target audience is. Then propose 3 or 4 possible titles and ask your evaluators which title they like best and why. All of the titles that you propose should naturally convey the essence of your presentation. After all, someone could love a title that has little or nothing to do with your presentation—and how helpful would that type of feedback to you?

Your final step in harnessing the power of feedback is to evaluate the responses you get. What rings true? What feedback can you disregard? What new insight came to you as a result of the feedback you have elicited? Did you learn anything that can help you make your personal "best choice" title even better?

You know your presentation and what you want to achieve with it better than anyone else. With that in mind, be open to feedback that could help you choose the best title and possibly improve it, but also trust yourself.

Almost every recipe can be made more healthful by changing
the method of preparation and by substituting or adding
more nutritious ingredients than those called for. Often only
slight revisions bring about tremendous improvements.

—*Adelle Davis,* Let's Cook It Right

Chapter Twenty-Eight

How This Chef Cooked Up a Tasty Title

To develop an effective title for a speech, workshop, or other creative work, it can help to treat your creative effort as a process. Ideally, you might like the perfect title to just pop out in one quick creative flash of inspiration. Typically, though, that's not the way that the mind works.

If you have a deep understanding of your target audience and are crystal clear about the core value of your speech, a powerful title could certainly come to you easily. But most often, you'll first need to do a certain amount of analytical thinking to set your creative wheels in motion. You might then generate several title possibilities before narrowing it down to the one that you feel would work best. Even then, you may need to analyze that "best choice" title and look for ways to tweak it and boost its impact, perhaps by applying one or more of the insights described in the Spices and Seasonings section of this book.

To give you a better sense of the kind of process you might use to develop an effective speech title, let me share with you the thought process I used in developing a title for one of my presentations. Your path to a powerful title may take other twists and turns than mine did. But I think that my experience will at least give you an idea of the analytical mindset and inquisitive nature you need to embrace to harness the full power of your creativity.

Earlier in my business life, I focused on helping business people and professionals develop their networking skills. To promote myself as a networking expert, I developed a showcase speech on networking. My initial working title for this speech was "How to Build Relationships that Bring You Business."

Overall, this seemed like a good working title. It highlighted business building, which was a major desire of my target audience. It related my topic of networking to that desire. And it seemed to clearly spell out how someone would benefit from attending my presentation.

To make this title even more compelling, though, I went deeper. I asked myself this: "What is it about networking that makes it seem like such a challenging and ineffective marketing approach to many business people?"

I came up with a number of answers. Sometimes business people were reluctant to strike up a conversation with strangers or felt uncomfortable selling themselves because they didn't want to seem too pushy. In other cases, they simply didn't know how to talk about their business in a compelling way or engage in a conversation that could open the door to a business opportunity. Even natural conversationalists often had trouble moving beyond chit-chat to launch business-building relationships. As a result of these different challenges, it could easily seem to take forever for business people to attract any new clients from all of their networking efforts.

I actually addressed all of these challenges in my showcase speech. Still, it would be a stretch to pack all of this into my title. That would be too unwieldy and possibly overwhelming. I had to narrow it down and find the issue that would resonate most with my target audience.

To do this, I asked myself another question: What is the most significant positive aspect of my particular approach to networking?

After giving this considerable thought, I came up with a one-word answer: speed. I showed my clients how to accelerate the whole process of launching business-building relationships. In doing this, I helped them to become more comfortable and skilled in initiating and engaging in profitable networking conversations. The deeper and more pervasive issue that I addressed, though, was their frustration with how long it took to generate business from their networking efforts.

Armed with this insight, I revised my working speech title to read as follows: "How to Launch Business-Building Relationships Faster Than You Thought Possible."

With this title, I not only highlighted a major desire of my target audience (business building), I addressed the main underlying frustration they most likely experienced in trying to achieve this desire (how long it took to see positive results from their networking efforts). This combination transformed my title from good to compelling.

Next, I asked myself how I might compact this title into a form that was shorter and had more punch to it. At the time, there was an emerging networking event concept known as speed networking, which was patterned after the model of speed dating that had been introduced a little earlier. Speed networking events created a structured environment in which you had a minute or two to pitch your business to other participants, exchange business cards, and then move on.

This whole experience might just as well have been called "hit-and-run networking," because that's what it felt like. It was fast. It was furious. But as a rule, the tight structure of this type of event just didn't allow enough time for you to have real conversations and make meaningful connections with the other participants.

As I tried to think of a short, punchy title I might give my networking presentation, I must admit that "speed networking" crossed my mind. I quickly rejected this idea, though, as what I taught was nothing like what people typically experienced at speed networking events and I didn't want my program to be associated with that kind of experience. I didn't encourage my audience members to try to set a land speed record for how many people they could meet at a networking event. My program was about showing people how to make meaningful connections and taking certain steps to speed up the building of trusting, supportive relationships.

With this mind, I finally decided to call my program Quick-Start Networking. This title didn't suggest that my networking approach required people to be fast talkers. Rather, it communicated that my program would show people how to get off to a quick start in learning the basics of effective networking, even if the whole networking game was new to them. At the same time, this title hinted at the notion that I would show my audience members how to launch relationships quickly.

This hint of meaning came into sharp focus when I combined my new short, snappy title with my longer working title, which became my subtitle. The result: "Quick-Start Networking: How to Launch Business-Building Relationships Faster than You Thought Possible."

The title captured people's attention, appealing to their need for speed without assuming the negative connotations of speed networking, while the subtitle clearly expressed the value of the program as it addressed the common frustration of how long it often takes to see tangible benefits from one's networking efforts.

You too can develop a compelling presentation title that conveys the essence of your message. You just need to be willing to dig deep into the needs and wants of your target audience and tailor your title to address them. It may take some poking around and exploration. But just realize that this is all part of the process of cooking up a title that arouses the appetite of those you most want to attract to your presentation.

You may grow old, even ugly, but if you are a good cook, people will always find a path to your door.

—*James Beard,* The James Beard Cookbook

Conclusion

Final Thoughts for Master Chefs

I hope that this book was, and continues to be, of help to you in crafting compelling titles for your presentations and other creative works. There is an old saying that if you build a better mouse trap, the world will beat a path to your door. The same might be said of speech titles. If you cook up a better speech title—and have a value-packed presentation to go with it—the world of your target audience will certainly beat a path to come hear what you have to say.

Armed with the insights and recipes in this book, you are now able to approach the process of creating a presentation title in a whole new way. In the past, you may have just scratched your head and asked "What in the world should I call this presentation?" Now you can ask a much more empowering question: "Which speech title recipe will serve me best?"

Rather than struggling to figure out how to create something from nothing, you can now begin by choosing from a whole menu of possibilities, each with its own step-by-step recipe to guide your creative process. As you are considering different recipes, don't think that you have to limit yourself to just one. Play with a few or even several. With your core speech topic in mind, create titles using a variety of recipes and see how they compare.

Looking at several possible speech titles, you can then make finer distinctions and get a greater sense of which title would resonate best with your target audience. In doing this, you might even see a way to transplant a key element from one title into another, revealing a creative possibility that you might never have discovered otherwise. And who knows—this might lead to the discovery of a whole new recipe. That can certainly happen when you are thinking like a master chef.

I approached the writing of this book as an intensely curious explorer, eager to uncover and communicate the answer to one simple question: What does it really take to create a compelling speech title? At first, I thought that I could answer this question in a short article. But with each page I wrote, I found more and more to say on the subject, much like the adventurer who reaches the crest of a hill only to find yet another hill to climb.

I've done my best in this book to summarize my research, discoveries and insights into the art of creating a compelling speech title. But if you come across other effective speech title recipes or are inspired to develop one or two new ones that work especially well for you, I'd love to hear about them. One chef to another.

Also, if you would like to share any success stories about the results you've achieved by applying what you've learned in this book, I would welcome those too. I may want to publish a revised and expanded edition of this book in the future, and any valuable input I receive from speakers who are out there crafting winning speech titles would only enrich the final product.

Just so you know, this is one case in which I don't place much credence in that old saying about too many cooks spoiling the broth. I'm always happy to learn from other master chefs who are brimming with creative ideas and finding new ways to whet people's appetite for a value-paced speech, presentation, or other creative work.

Your title is your appetizer; your presentation is your main course. Best of luck in delighting and captivating your target audience with both.

You can contact me at:

Sam Wieder
235 Hawksworth Road
Greensburg, PA 15601
sam@CommandingConfidence.com

This is my invariable advice to people: Learn how to cook—try new recipes, learn from your mistakes, be fearless, and above all have fun!

—*Julia Child*, My Life in France

Appendix One: Summary of Recipes

Pain and Problems

Problem Resolution:
Overcome Writer's Block

Problem Prevention:
Avoid Costly Lawsuits

Firing Up Frustration:
Stop Struggling with Marketing

Creating Urgency

Model 1: Act now or lose
Specialize or Starve

Model 2: Act now or a problem will get worse
How to Keep Small Disagreements from Destroying Your Relationships

Model 3: Act now and win
How to prepare now for record sales next year

Model 4: Now is an especially good time to act
Boost Your Sales to Today's Top Growth Industry

Concise and Catchy Main Titles

Power Pair:
Financial Fitness

The Triple:
Speak with Impact
Master Your Money

Call to Action:
Focus on What Counts

Action Call to Result:
Walk and Get Fit

Double Shot of Expressiveness

Double Benefits:
Build Your Network and Boost Your Sales

Achievement and Benefit:
How to Write a Book that Gives You Expert Status

Show the benefit, add a qualifier:
Lose Weight without Giving Up the Foods You Love

Solve a problem, show the result:
How to Stop Worrying and Start Living
(Dale Carnegie book title)

Contrast before and after:
How to Turn Struggling Students into Star Learners

Double Negative:
Interviewing Mistakes that will Cost You the Job

Add a measure of value

Point to underlying reasons:
The 5 Reasons that Office Workers Suffer with Chronic Low Back Pain
The 7 Habits of Highly Effective People (Steven Covey)

Showcase mistakes:
The 6 Mistakes that Cause Restaurants to Lose Customers

Step up your speech title:
The 7 Steps to Landing Your Dream Job

Mix in your method

Method First:
How to Use Social Media to Attract Joint Venture Partners

Method Second:
How to Attract Clients Through Public Speaking

Advanced Recipes

Metaphor:
How to Win in the Game of Business
Dig Your Well Before You're Thirsty (Harvey MacKay)

Fairy Tales/Children's Stories:
Lessons from Rip Van Winkle: How to Finally Get a Good Night's Sleep

Catch Phrases:
Live Long and Prosper: How to Plan for a Financially Secure Retirement

Curious Combo:
Emotional Intelligence (Daniel Goleman book title)
Purple Cow: Transform Your Business by Being Remarkable (Seth Godin book title)

Shocking Statement:
People are idiots and I can prove it: The 10 Ways You are Sabotaging Yourself and How You Can Overcome Them (Larry Winget book title)

Contrarian Statement:
Toss Your To-Do List and Double Your Productivity

Tap your experience to create your signature dish:
Enhance Your Presentation: What I Learned from Winning 29 Emmys that Speakers Need to Know (Workshop Title by Bill Stainton)

Appendix Two:
Methods of Spicing Up Your Title

Use vital verbs:
Conquer Your Fear
Unleash Your Potential

Stimulate the senses:
Watch Your Sales Soar (visual)
Applaud Their Successes (auditory)
Inspire Your Team (feeling)

Alliteration:
Make Money in the Market
Ten Tactics for Speaking Success

Rhyme:
How Food Affects Your Mood
Make Money from Being Funny

Word Play:
Beat Burnout Before...You are Toast
(Wellness Expert Jan Krouskop)

Everything's Coming Up Neurosis
(Motivational Humorist Michael Broome)

Rhythm/Parallel Construction:
Write Your Book to Boost Your Credibility
Cook Like a Chef, Dine Like a King

Spice it up with specificity:
Double Your Energy
Accomplish Twice as Much in Half the Time
How to Get Thousands in Free Publicity

Feed their need for speed:
How to Lose 10 Pounds in 30 Days
Triple Your Reading Speed
How to Speed Up Your Sales Cycle

Recommended Resources

Advertising Headlines to Make Your Rich, David Garfinkel, Morgan James Publishing, Garden City, NY, 2006.

Cash Copy: How To Offer Your Products and Services So Your Prospects Buy Them...Now, Dr. Jeffrey Lant, JLA Publications, Cambridge, MA, 1992.

The Copywriter's Handbook: A Step-by-Step Guide to Writing Copy That Sells, Robert W. Bly, Henry Holt and Company, New York, 1985, 2005.

The Elements of Style, William Strunk, Jr. and E.B. White, The MacMillan Company, New York, 1972.

Phrases That Sell, Edward Werz and Sally Germain, Contemporary Books, Chicago, 1998

Pop! Create the Perfect Pitch, Title, and Tagline for Anything, Sam Horn, Penguin Group, New York, 2006.

Words That Sell, Richard Bayan, McGraw-Hill, New York, 2006

Public Speaking Organizations:

National Speakers Association (www.nsaspeaker.org) – the premier association for experts who speak professionally.

Toastmasters International (www.toastmasters.org) – an educational organization that helps members develop their public speaking and leadership skills.

About the Author

Sam Wieder has coached hundreds of speakers, including high school and college students, consulting professionals, business executives, and professional speakers. He works with both executives who want to speak with greater confidence and impact and professionals who want to attract clients through public speaking.

Active in the world of public speaking for over 30 years, Sam is a past president of the Pittsburgh chapter of the National Speakers Association and a former high school speech and debate coach in the National Forensic League. He has taught college-level business communication classes, coordinated educational events for speakers, and has been recognized by Toastmasters International as a Distinguished Toastmaster. He has presented speeches and workshops in the U.S., Canada, and Europe.

Understanding the influential power of language, Sam is a Certified Trainer of Neuro-linguistic Programming and has an 8-year background as a professional marketing writer. He has written special-occasion poetry and enjoys channeling his poet's sense of rhythm and rhyme into his own speech and seminar titles. He has also edited and recipe-tested an actual cook book, which in part inspired him to write this cook book for speakers.

To learn more about Sam and his services, visit his web site at: www.CommandingConfidence.com.